One-Way Relationships

ALFRED ELLS

THOMAS NELSON PUBLISHERS
Nashville

Published in Nashville, Tennessee, by Thomas Nelson, Inc., and distributed in Canada by Lawson Falle, Ltd., Cambridge, Ontario.

Printed in the United States of America.

Unless otherwise noted, Scripture quotations are from the NEW KING JAMES VERSION of the Bible. Copyright © 1979, 1980, 1982, Thomas Nelson, Inc., Publishers.

Scripture quotations noted NASB are from THE NEW AMERICAN STANDARD BIBLE, Copyright © 1960, 1962, 1963, 1968, 1971, 1973, 1972, 1975, 1977 by The Lockman Foundation and are used by permission.

Scripture quotations noted NIV are from The Holy Bible: NEW INTERNATIONAL VERSION. Copyright © 1978 by the New York International Bible Society. Used by permission of Zondervan Bible Publishers.

This book contains true stories. Several individuals granted full permission to use their specific profiles to help others. All other identities are concealed as composites of several case histories.

Library of Congress Cataloging-in-Publication information
Ells, Alfred.
    One-way relationships / Alfred Ells.
    ISBN 0-8407-3142-6
    1. Codependents—Religious life. 2. Co-dependency (Psychology)-
-Religious aspects—Christianity. I. Title.
BV4596.C57E45   1990
248.8′6—dc20   89-78171
                                        CIP

1 2 3 4 5 — 94 93 92 91 90

Contents

Dedication   **v**
Acknowledgments   **vii**
Foreword   **ix**
Introduction   **xi**

1   The Truth about One-Way Relationships   **17**

2   Am I to Blame for All the Problems?   **33**

3   How to Deal with the Other Person
   in a One-Way Relationship   **43**

4   Introducing Codependency: The New Term
   for the Root Problem in Relationships   **53**

5   Why Are Codependents Codependent?   **67**

6   The Remarkable Power of Imprinting   **79**

7   The Imprint of Codependency Began
   in Your Family   **91**

8   What You Lose Can Change Your Life   **113**

9   You're Only as Sick as Your Secrets
   and Shame   **129**

10   A Wounded Heart's Cry for Love   **143**

11 How to Heal Your Wounds **159**

12 How to Face Their Anger and Win **169**

13 Intimacy Can Cause or Cure
       Codependency **187**

14 How to Prevent Codependency **199**

15 Who Is Your God? **215**

To my families:
Susan, my wife
Missy
Matt
Andrew
Katie

and

Mom and Dad
Loren
Michael
Gary
Larry
Kathy
Diane
Robert

Acknowledgments

MY GRATITUDE AND THANKS to the many people who have helped me put this book together. My friend, Michael Clifford, had the vision. He stirred me to action and got the ball rolling. David Manuel told me I could write, and Jamie Buckingham said I needed to write.

The staff of Samaritan Counseling Center and Hope Community have all supported me. Judy Wakefield has been an angel. She deciphered the scratchy handwriting and typed the cut and pasted pages of manuscript. Tim, Susan, Edye, René, Diane, Larry, and Rudy were all there in prayer and encouragement.

My deepest gratitude to Sarah Coleman, my editor, and Susan, my wife. They believed in me, prayed for me, and told me I could do it. Sarah's support and expertise carried me through the times of doubt. Susan's love and care made the long days and early morning hours bearable.

But Jesus made it all possible. He's guided me through the mazes of people's lives and problems to witness how He brings hope and healing.

Foreword

I FIRST MET Al Ells at a workshop on compulsive-addictive behavior. He impressed me by his transparency and the quiet confidence that he expressed in helping people. He clearly answers the often asked questions of "What is wrong with me? Why don't the relationships in my life work?"

As an author and person concerned with the issues of women, I believe this book will be a touchstone and reminder that God is *the* proven source of strength. He is integrity and will bring the healing process lovingly and thoroughly. He alone can fill the empty places in life if people are willing to apply these professional and spiritual truths.

Ells writes distinctly. Relevant to the addictions of alcohol, food, prescription drugs, and life's painful one-way relationships. He teaches specific prayer steps to open unhealed wounds, uncover deeply buried grief, and resolve those unfinished areas of the past.

The heart of *One-Way Relationships* activated in my mind a verse from the Bible:

You show that you are a letter from Christ, the result of our ministry, written not with ink but with the spirit of the living God, not on the tablets of stone but on tablets of human hearts. 2 Corinthians 3:3 (NIV)

These pages are a letter, written to each reader. A letter filled with the answers that can restore broken relationships. A letter to those who suffer from the disease and afflictions of codependency. A life-changing letter of hope and healing.

Sandra Simpson LeSourd
Author of *The Compulsive Woman*

Introduction

IT CAME TO ME the moment I woke up. I'm in a one-way relationship with my dad. That is why I've struggled with our relationship for such a long time. Vacillating between anger and apologies, between pursuing him and ignoring him. At times I have not contacted him for months, just waited for his call, which never came. I've invited him for Thanksgiving dinner and been hurt when he did not show—again! My kids wonder why Grandpa has never been to our home and why he has never given them Christmas presents. My brothers say, "That's just the way he is," but I have a hard time accepting it.

I've cried, prayed, given up, and then tried again. It still comes out the same—I give and he takes; I risk and he plays it safe; I reach out, wondering if he really cares as much as I do.

I'm a marriage and family therapist who is having to walk the same path to God's healing as my clients. Struggling with my own one-way relationship has made me acutely aware of the countless others who are in the same trap. They come in different shapes and sizes and from varied cultures and ethnic backgrounds, but the dynamic is the same: one person seeming to love, give, or care more than the other.

Frequently a housewife reads all the right books and prays fervently for her marriage, but her husband remains too glued to the television set to talk to her. She expends all the energy to make the marriage work. He cashes in on the dividends.

Or a daughter calls daily and listens to Mom's problems, but is never asked how she feels. Is what she does for her mother all that matters? Is she really loved?

Enter the parents who repeatedly go into debt to rescue an addicted son who can't—or won't—kick the cocaine habit. He takes and takes, giving only heartbreak in return.

Maybe it is a friend who can never seem to do anything for herself. She's always asking you to do it for her and you can't seem to refuse. You feel you are being taken advantage of, but are afraid to say no because it might hurt her feelings or increase the heavy emotional baggage she complains she carries.

This is a book for all who struggle in relationships that feel unbalanced or one-sided. This is a book for marrieds, singles, grandparents, friends, and even children. This is a book for those of you who want profound changes in your lives and relationships. Change is often difficult and painful, but rewarding.

The awareness of my one-way relationship with my father brought pain, but it resulted in healing. Change requires a fearless commitment to reality, to the truth. I did not want to face the fact that my dad cared less about the relationship. I wanted him to desire it as much as or even more than I did.

Change requires the courage to face ourselves before we face others. I needed to see what it was in me that wanted, even demanded, a relationship that the other person cared nothing about. I don't like having to examine myself like this. I tend either to avoid any responsibility for change or to take on too much guilt to be able to change.

It takes courage for all of us to look deeply enough inside to sort out the balanced and real truth about ourselves, especially regarding the root issues of our lives that have determined how we relate to others. Stripping back the layers from yesterday is painful.

I was still trying to recapture the past in my one-way relationship; I was emotionally unfinished with it. When the past is not fully resolved, it is inevitably relived in the present. I needed to face my past, but doing it alone was not possible. Change requires the faith and humility to ask for help when what we see in ourselves is ugly and painful. The anonymous programs have a step asserting that it takes "a power greater than ourselves" to restore us to sanity.

Hope and healing came when I shared with God and others what I saw in myself. It took my willingness and His power to change.

Will is the desire and power is the ability of willpower. Many chapters of this book have prayer steps to test and guide your willingness to receive His power. You may have a deep faith in Christ as I do, or you may be doubtful or searching. If you are, don't let this interfere with your being healed. Try the prayer steps. God reveals Himself to those who seek Him. Risk it as we explore together the answers to our one-way relationships.

Chapter 1

One-way relationships—
when you love, care, and give
too much—
are a problem but,
paradoxically,
also an opportunity.

☐ The Truth about One-Way Relationships

IS IT REALLY GOOD to love, care, or give more than the other person in a relationship? I've struggled with this question for some time. My Christian background and belief say it's better to love than be loved, more blessed to give than receive. And something deep inside affirms that sacrificial love is the greatest power in the universe for "greater love hath no man than he lay down his life for his friend."

Yet, my experience shows that a one-way or sacrificially loving relationship rarely works well. Our counseling center works daily with marriages that are in trouble because one of the partners gives, cares, or loves more than the other. My own parents ended up separated after twenty-five years of battling the effects of a one-way relationship. There are countless spouses, usually wives of alcoholics and addicts, who have gone the extra mile of giving, caring, and loving. All to no avail. They are still abused, and the relationship is worse than before. Their sacrificial love doesn't work.

It also isn't working for the children of these marriages. A new wave of support groups has evolved all over the country in the past few years for adult children who grew up in alcoholic families. These children ask for help because they recognize that their relationships and lives aren't working. They suffer the effects of a dysfunctional home environment, repeating failed relationships in epidemic numbers. Many are deeply wounded and puzzled over how they ended up marrying and taking care of an alcoholic when it was the last thing they wanted to do.

But this is just the tip of the iceberg. We are continually confronted with more parents putting more worry into their wayward children than ever before. Parents who give, care, and love in extra measure to try to get their kids off drugs, off the streets, or onto the road of responsibility. It appears that the more they give, the less it helps. It is not unusual to see able-bodied twenty- and even thirty-year-olds living in their parents' homes and not working. They promise to get a job and become responsible but rarely follow through. Mom and Dad agonize over the situation but keep giving and giving, supporting the children when they should be supporting themselves. We now have "Tough Love" groups for parents to help them face this ineffective one-way pattern of relating.

In countless other relationships and love affairs, one person is the giver and the other the taker. In our secular society infidelity is commonplace and rationalized even though it is a self-centered getting at another's expense. The faithful spouse continues giving faithfulness while the cheater takes full advantage and doesn't return the desired faithfulness.

It's a common saying that men give love in order to get sex while women give sex in order to get love. Our obsession with sex and love has led to an unprecedented number of women who have been cheated on, molested, raped, or sexually abused. Incest is not uncommon. Yet many wives remain loyal to lustful husbands, continuing to love, care, and give despite their mate's penchant for pornography, flirtation, prostitution, abuse, and infidelity. Is this one-sided loyalty healthy? Does it work? Is the best way to deal with the unfairness and sickness just to keep on giving? The question is compounded in the escalating cycles of abuse.

What about the well-known pattern of the wife who takes care of the kids, cooks the meals, cleans the house, and runs the household while the husband comes home late, refuses to help with the kids, watches TV instead of talking, then gets angry when she won't give him sex? She complains that the relationship is one-way. She gives, cares, takes responsibility, and loves while he gives little and demands much.

Is the apparent unfairness of this healthy? Is her one-way giving really good for the relationship? The facts validate that the more one gives, the more the other takes and the less the relationship is helped. As a matter of fact, this one-sided sacrificial loving often makes things worse.

How then can it be better to love than be loved, give than receive, when it doesn't really improve or change things? The answer became clearer when Sally came to me for counseling.

Tears streamed down her face, leaving black streaks of mascara on her cheeks. Twisting a tissue she said, "I don't understand how this can be happening to me again. This is the second time someone I've loved has been unfaithful to me."

Even through the tears it was easy to see that Sally was a very attractive woman, one that men would easily find desirable. However, Phil had cheated on her with her best friend. Sally was shattered, and the marriage was on shaky ground.

Puzzled, I asked her what had gone wrong.

"I don't know. Our sex life was tremendous. We made love four or five times a week. I did everything I could to please him. I fixed his meals, washed his clothes, and kept the house clean. I desperately tried to make the marriage work. I didn't want to fail again. I even sent my daughter, Kathy, to live with my mom because she made Phil nervous. I just don't understand what more a man could want from me."

"Was it like this in your first marriage?" I asked.

Startled, she looked up through her tears. "I don't know. Bob and I were childhood sweethearts, and I got pregnant. My home life wasn't the greatest so I couldn't wait to marry Bob and have our own family. He had a high-pressure job, so I tried to make things as comfortable for him as I could. I hated it when he came home later and later with the smell of alcohol on his breath."

"Bob liked to drink?"

"Oh, yes. I used to meet him at his favorite place until our first child was born. Maybe if I hadn't stopped meeting him, he would never have become involved with 'her' and divorced me."

Tears once again erupted and cascaded heavily down her face. Married twice to men who cheated on her, she was now assuming all the guilt and blame. Was she really to blame? I questioned further.

"What was your home like when you were growing up?"

"Dad was always gone and Mom was always upset. We had to be really quiet when he was home, or else he would blow up and hit us or Mom. I tried to protect my younger brothers and sisters from the endless fights, but it was hard to do."

"Both your parents are still alive?"

"No. Mom is, but Dad died four years ago. I moved her closer to me after Dad's death, and I check in with her every day to make sure she's all right. She's having a hard time right now with her back, and her neighbors are giving her fits. I cook meals for her and do everything I can to make her comfortable."

"Have you always taken such good care of your mom?"

"Oh, yes. I have always been the one she could count on. She would share with me the problems she had with Dad. She told me I was a good listener. It meant a lot to her to have a daughter who cared and listened."

"Have you also been caring and a good listener with your husbands?"

"Bob told me I was a good listener. He was moody and had a lot of problems with his family and job. It made him feel better when I listened to him and massaged his shoulders."

"What about Phil?"

"I guess so. After Bob left me I got a job as Phil's secretary. He complained about his wife never understanding him and always wanting to control everything. I listened to him and tried to help. We became involved with each other before I realized what was happening."

"It sounds like you care a lot about others. Does anyone ever listen to you or care for you?"

The sobs became an audible wail. She grieved over the

deep hurt of never really being cared for or listened to even though she had given so much. Then she recovered her composure, becoming silent and reflective.

I knew what Sally's problem was—I had the answer to her dilemma. Sally is a giver, a caretaker, a one-sided lover. She takes care of everybody: Mom, husbands, brothers, sisters, and even an old woman next door. She loves sacrificially at her own expense. She listens to everyone's problems though few pay attention to hers. Yet these appearances do not reveal a spiritual depth of loving.

Sally was not a truly sacrificial lover. She was a casualty of misunderstood love. Her loving was conditional, not sacrificial. True love is patient, kind, not envious or self-seeking. Sally was patient and kind, but deep down she was also envious and self-seeking—envious of those who received so much love and attention, self-seeking because she really loved in order to be loved. She was loving and giving, all the while hoping she would get it back. Sally was doing what most of us do when there is a lack of love in our own lives. We do something to get our need for love met.

Sally had always been the one who gave to others. The pattern was set early in the childhood relationship with her mom. Sally didn't know how to receive love, only how to give it. She also, however, wanted the love she never got. Somewhere along the way, maybe even from the very beginning, she learned that the only way to get love was to give it. She then started giving in order to get. All of us do this to some degree. It comes naturally. We're nice to others so that they will be nice to us. We're even taught by our parents to "smile so people will like you." We have all learned the oldest ethic of doing for others so they will do for us—good deeds, kindness, even love.

Giving for the Wrong Reason

Children learn quickly what to do to get their needs met. The only way to get attention or love in Sally's family was for her to give it first. Her mother was needy. She had a difficult relationship with Sally's dad. Sally gave Mom the listening ear and caring that her mom needed from Dad. She fulfilled the emotional needs that Dad didn't fill. It was as though Sally became Mom's answer to the pain of a difficult marriage. This further complicated Sally's life by teaching her to take on the identity of a fixer. Sally needed to be needed by someone in order to feel good about herself. She assumed the classic role of a fixer. Her relationships were always based on someone else having a need and her needing to help them. She married unhealthy, needy men because they appealed to her need to be needed by someone. Sally was victimized by her own style of giving, loving, and caring. Her sacrificial loving was really an attempt to get love by giving.

Because of her, I now understood my own dilemma. It can be good or bad to love, care, or give more than the other person. It's the motive behind the giving that is so important. *It is more blessed to give than receive when you don't give to receive. It's better to love than be loved when you don't love in order to be loved.* Love is a good virtue, as are tenderness, kindness, and caring for others. These qualities make life and relationships worthwhile. But these virtues must stem from a pure heart where we are giving not to get, loving not to be loved, and caring not to be cared for. Sacrificial, unconditional love can work when there are no strings attached, when nothing muddies the waters or distorts the outcome. The blessing comes from the giving only, not from the receiving.

Unhealthy sacrificial love is not really sacrificial; it's self-serving. It's giving, caring, or loving because we want something in return. We want more love or we want someone to change or we want to protect ourselves and have our fears quieted. This mixture of motives is what makes truly sacrificial or unconditional love so hard to come by. It's also why most seemingly sacrificial one-way relationships don't work. Few of us have ever loved another unconditionally. Probably still fewer of us have ever truly been loved unconditionally by anyone. Sacrificial, unconditional love can change us and others. It can melt our hearts, get past our defenses, and encourage us to risk. It can make up for the love never given or the uncaring that we have suffered. But most love is not sacrificial. It is selfish. Most love is conditional, not free. It really comes from a need to get, not a desire to give.

As a child Sally never received the unconditional love she needed from Mom or Dad. Dad was absent; Mom, preoccupied with her own problems. The only way Sally got attention, love, or affection was to listen to Mom's problems with Dad. Her mom often said, "I don't know what I would do without you, honey. You're the only bright spot in my life. You always give me hope when I talk to you."

Sally learned quickly how to get by giving. But it never worked for long. The more she gave, the less she got and the hungrier she became. She was trapped in an unhealthy pattern of one-way relationships in which it is not more blessed to give than to receive. Her motives became mixed and her love distorted. What she thought unselfish was really self-serving. It's hard to give and not get back. It's difficult to love without return. It's frustrating to pick up responsibilities that others refuse to carry. We give more with less satisfaction. There is no mutuality. This lack leads quickly to offense and feelings of hurt, fear, or self-doubt. We soon give more so we don't get hurt again. Or we demand more because the hurt has turned to anger or fear. We keep hoping, even demanding, that the other person will change, all the while thinking that we are the loving one, caring or giving unconditionally and sacrificially.

Sally is not alone in her self-defeating trap of one-way relating. Thousands of wounded women and men, caught in painful dating, marriage, friendship, business, or family relationships don't understand why the relationship is not working, though they desperately keep trying. Many, like Sally, love too much in order to be loved, give or care too much in order to be cared about.

Others, however, love for a different reason. Instead of loving to be loved, they love in order to avoid their own pain and quiet their inner fears. Loving, caring, or giving so that we don't hurt is also a part of one-way relationships. Wives or loved ones of addicts know this pattern well. And parents who love, protect, and want the best for their children are also especially vulnerable.

When someone we love is hurting for any reason, it hurts us also because we see how everything that is good is being destroyed. Additional hurt comes through rejection or violation of our trust and care. It may even bother us because it damages our pride and reputation. Anyone who has to deal with an emotionally troubled or out-of-control loved one will have difficulty avoiding entrapment in an unhealthy one-way relationship. Betty is an example.

In her seventies, well dressed, and walking with the aid of a cane, Betty was obviously uncomfortable and acted as though she really didn't want counseling. Hesitantly, she said, "It's my daughter."

"What about your daughter?" I asked in response.

"Bill thinks I ought to talk to you about our daughter."

I immediately sensed the problem but felt I should continue probing. "What makes Bill think we need to talk about your daughter?"

"He thinks I need to let go."

"Let go of what?"

"Let go of my daughter. She is having trouble again in her marriage, and I don't want it to fail like the others. She's a very sensitive child and can't take much pressure."

"Why does Bill think you need to let go?"

"Because I worry day and night about her, and the doctor has told me I need to rest or I'll have another heart attack."

"What about you? Do you think you need to let go?"

"Somebody has to help her. I pray for her all the time, but things are not getting any better. I really came hoping you could help her somehow."

My heart ached for Betty. She wanted my help in "fixing" her daughter's marriage, thinking that would solve her own pain.

"Betty, I can't help your daughter, but I can help you.

That is, if you're willing to see how you're making your daughter's problems worse."

This shocked Betty, but it caught her attention. For the first time she looked inside herself—worried, anxious, over-protective, and also feeling guilty. In this one-way relationship, Betty cared more about her daughter's problems than about her daughter.

Parents who have out-of-control or "problem" children experience the same inner pain Betty faces. "Is it my fault? What did I do wrong? If I don't protect, control, or do something, what will happen? Should I do more? Less? An out-of-control, emotionally lost, or unsuccessful child will provoke the same fear and guilt in all caring parents. It's hard to set limits on caring when you love. It's complicated to know when to let go and let God enter the scene.

Families with learning disabled or handicapped children face this challenge on a daily basis. How much should be expected? How much protection is sufficient? Applying pressure to perform beyond ability may result in wounds that cause even more problems. However, the lack of enough challenge leads to overprotection and unnecessary limitations. Parenting is difficult. Children not measuring up to expectations or society's standards provoke us to protect, control, rescue, or punish. This is another setup for unhealthy one-way relationship patterns.

The same is true for anyone closely involved with an addicted person. Addicts are out of control, under the influence of something more powerful than themselves. This applies whether the addiction is to food, alcohol, drugs, sex, pornography, music, or love. The lack of control in the addict provokes a dominant need to control the caring loved one. The parent, wife, husband, child, or friend of an addict becomes fearful, desperate, and hurt. We try to control the situation so that we won't hurt. This makes relationships with someone who is addicted very difficult because their bondage is also our pain. Never seeing the need to fix herself, Betty tried to alter the situation of her forty-four-year-old daughter to ease her own pain.

Instead of facing her problems, rooted in the past, Betty focused on running interference for her daughter. She, like most of us, was emotionally unfinished with her own beginning. Because she had never dealt with her mother's overprotection and the fears it bred, fear and guilt ruled her life as well as her relationship with her daughter. Her caring was tainted by guilt and motivated by fear. What she thought was sacrificial caring was really a self-serving attempt to ease her fears and appease her personal guilt.

Healthy Caring

Does that mean she didn't care at all or that she shouldn't try to help? Certainly not. Any loving parent would do the same. Betty just cared too much; she tried to help in ways that weren't helpful. Betty had a pattern of overprotectiveness and control. *Healthy caring seeks the best for the object of one's care.* This principle of seeking the best for another recognizes that we are always the answer to our own pain and problems. Betty's daughter is herself the answer to her own marital discord. Betty's protectiveness was keeping her daughter dependent and emotionally tied to maternal apron strings, and this, in turn, was a major problem in the daughter's marriage. The attachment was so strong that it prevented any bonding between husband and wife. Betty was making the problems worse.

Trying to change others to prevent our hurt only causes more pain. This doesn't mean we should never hope for change or share the truth of the need for change, but it does mean we should never become preoccupied with the problems and lack of change. Betty's preoccupation mirrored her own need for change rather than reflecting care, love, and concern for her daughter.

The loved ones of an addicted or troubled person need to evaluate their emotions solemnly in light of this principle. Failure to do so spawns many self-defeating one-way relationships that work for no one. This pattern of one-sidedness, preoccupied as it is with the shortcomings of the other party, is at the heart of most marriage problems. Each partner becomes too preoccupied with the other's faults to admit his or her own.

The partners may change, but the patterns are comparable and the rhetoric similar.

"You never help me with the kids or anything else. I'm tired of having to do it all myself. You never give me any support and I'm getting tired of this. Do you understand?"

Obviously angry, Marilyn began another marriage counseling session with a blistering accusation against her husband, Tim.

"Well, you're no day at the beach either," he retorted, "and I'm fed up with your nagging and complaining. That's all you ever do."

"If you'd do something to help for a change, I wouldn't have to nag you. But all you do is come home late and plop yourself down in front of the TV while I have to fix dinner, feed the kids, and get them ready for bed."

"If you'd get off my back, I might help."

They were a picture of deadlocked wedlock. The more she complained, the more he defended. At other times he promised to help, but he rarely followed through, making her even more angry.

Marilyn was trying to keep up with a six-month-old baby and a two-year-old toddler while Tim was struggling in a highly competitive market and a pressure-cooker job. Neither could see the other's dilemma. An unhealthy one-way relationship pattern was in the making.

As Marilyn did more and complained more, Tim defended more and did less. The cycle continued: Tim withdrew and ignored her and her pleas for help. She, in turn, became more angry, hurt, and demanding. Each felt victimized, certain that if only the other would change, everything would be all right.

Marilyn's friends realized that she was the more giving and offered conflicting advice. "I wouldn't lift a finger for him. He's a creep. Quit enabling him and let him fix his own dinner," a close neighbor admonished.

"You need to ask him to help in a nice way. If you keep loving and serving him, he'll change and things will be better," her Bible study leader encouraged.

Faced with the choice of either stopping her service or continuing or even increasing it with a nicer attitude, she felt trapped. She could do nothing. One-way relationships always ambush us when our loving, caring, or giving is wrongly motivated. Marilyn was angry but not just with Tim. She was angry with life. Although passive and not much help, Tim was not the root problem; he only added fuel to an existing fire.

Marilyn came from a stable but unhealthy family background. Dad was usually gone and Mom ran the show. But Mom directed traffic with a lot of control and criticism. Dad was a nice guy who tried to stay out of Mom's way. Marilyn inevitably learned to operate in an angry, demanding way just as her mother had. She took care of the house because she had to and got angry when it wasn't clean or done right. She got mad at herself and everyone else who contributed to the daily mess. The treatment she gave others was a carbon copy of her mother's. Anger was what motivated her to action. Her giving and serving were more a reflection of her anger and uptightness than of her love, care, and concern for herself, her family, and her home.

Interestingly, Tim's mom was much like Marilyn's in style, and he responded to his wife just as he had to his mother. Tim's own past was as unresolved as Marilyn's. Both needed to accept responsibility for inner change rather than being preoccupied with reshaping the other. Marilyn was still harboring anger and hurt against her mom. She was unknowingly resentful of her dad for never helping and therefore causing her mother's anger.

Most marriage problems are one-way relationship problems. Loving, caring, or giving too much for the wrong reason rarely works. Both marriage partners usually contribute to the pattern and suffer the effects. The first step toward a healthy relationship is to acknowledge the need for change—change in ourselves, not just the other person.

Another illustration is my friend who has come to realize that she is the answer to her own pain and that her one-way pattern of relating is unhealthy. She has been loving, caring, and giving too much for the wrong reasons. She is the original nice person. Have you ever known someone who is nice all the time? No matter what happens or what is done, the reaction is predictably sweet. Everybody knows someone like this. My friend never says anything mean, and I can't recall her ever being critical or angry. Her husband is rude and disagreeable, but she rarely flares up or retaliates.

I used to think she was a saint until her husband told me one day that she threw dishes at him in a rage. I couldn't imagine her doing such a thing until she confirmed it by saying, "Every now and then he hurts me so badly, I just blow up inside and lose control. Afterward I feel so guilty. I'm afraid he'll leave me, so I try to make up for it by being as nice as I can. I wish I weren't so mean."

As we talked, she shared more of her inner fears and insecurities. Raised in a difficult home environment, she always tried to please her dad so that he wouldn't be angry with her. She vowed to be nice in order to avert anger and criticism. Her niceness became a defense mechanism. Ever notice how hard it is to be angry with a nice person? Overly nice pleasers are deadly serious about being charming and likable, which makes them setups for unhealthy one-way relationships. Typically, she avoided disagreement or confrontation with her husband. When a conflict arose, her tendency was to avoid the issue or yield and go along with him just to "keep the peace." Pleasers want to please. To do it, they will promise the impractical and then be unable to follow through. She handled the checkbook even though she was too busy and not good at numbers. If the bank account was overdrawn, he would become angry and frustrated with her. His anger and disapproval were the very responses she was attempting to avoid. The angrier he got, the more fearful she became and the more mistakes she made, thus making him even more hostile. She then felt victimized, never really seeing the self-defeating pattern that her desire to please, coupled with her fear of him, was creating since she always managed to blame herself. It was a vicious cycle of defeat.

Pleasers are fearful—afraid of rejection and disapproval. Many had critical or negative parents. They figured out early that the way to keep from being wounded was to learn to please. They learned to please to win love and avoid pain. Adult one-way relating stems from the wounds and fears of childhood that need healing. Because pleasers are self-protective, they have a hard time loving unconditionally. Those who try to please others cause distortion of love because the motive is sick. They love to be loved and avoid pain. They give to get. They care in order to be cared about.

The problem with one-way relationships is that they are usually a reflection of our damaged ability to love rather than a proof of true love or rightful giving. *One-way relationships are usually a cause or result of impure love, not an indication of true, unconditional love.* It's in the motive for our loving, caring, or giving that truth is revealed. We can give without loving and we can love by giving. People who love too much usually want and need too much to be loved. Those who care too much really need care for their own fears and pain. Those who want to please are desperately trying to accept themselves by being accepted by others.

One-way relationships are a problem but, paradoxically, an opportunity. We are the problem, and the opportunity is God's!

One-way relationships can drive us to what we really need. We hold the answers to our own pain and problems. Recognizing that we are in a one-way relationship can free us to take a deeper look at ourselves and our need to be loved. It will enable us to receive God's unconditional, sacrificial, healthy, one-way loving. Acknowledging our deep neediness can prepare us for receiving His abundant provision.

Chapter 2

Denial soothes our senses but
keeps us in bondage.
The truth hurts in a
one-way relationship,
but it will set you free.

2   Am I to Blame for All the Problems?

"I FEEL LIKE it's all my fault. There must be something I'm not doing right. Yet, I find myself getting mad and blaming him for the problems and then feeling guilty afterward. Am I really to blame?"

This is how Sally began another one of her counseling sessions with me. Deep down Sally thought she was the problem. If only she could love, care, or give enough, then her husband would be happy. She had deep insecurities and took all the responsibility for the problem on herself. Then when he didn't respond to her giving, she became angry, convinced that it was really all his fault! After the anger passed, her self-doubts returned. Sally's confusion and vacillation over who was really to blame is characteristic of a one-way relationship. She was sharing openly what most of us in a one-way relationship inwardly experience. We wonder not only why our loving, caring, and giving aren't working but who is at fault for its failure. Who's to blame for all this pain and difficulty?

Few people in a one-way relationship sort out and apportion the blame. They vacillate within or fight back and forth over who's right and who's wrong. Families and friends provide little help. They say either it's all the fault of one for not loving, caring, or giving enough or it's all the other's fault and you're letting him or her do this to you. Either way, you'll feel like you're to blame. But relationships are a complex dynamic of two people, not just one. Both contribute to the strengths and weaknesses. Both contribute to the problem.

Each is a part of the reason the one-way relationship pattern continues to be unhealthy. It's not just one person's fault. Since each continues to act and react according to the existing negative pattern, nothing changes. Or if it does change, it only takes a turn for the worse.

Both are to blame for perpetuating the problem, but nothing is likely to change until one or both work through the blame issue and arrive at a healthy appraisal of what's really wrong and what needs to be done about it. When the blame is worked through in a positive manner, the contribution of each is clearly seen.

Avoiding Unhealthy Blame

Unhealthy blame does not really try to see the matter in an unbiased, realistic way. Rather it attempts to assign fault in a judgmental way. Unhealthy blame has a punishing flavor. It is focused on the past and what happened then rather than on the future and what needs to change.

Blame, when rightly affixed, pinpoints responsibility for change. It causes us to see truly how each person is contributing to the problem and what changes each must make to enhance the relationship. This healthy blame is really an uncovering of the truth about both people and the way they relate to each other. It's not a negative accusation of faults but rather a truthful revelation for both. As long as we're blaming ourselves or the other person, we're stuck, and nothing will change. If we refuse blame, we are stuck in judgment, anger, and self-righteousness, perhaps even self-pity and victimization. If we blame ourselves, we are condemned to defeat and depression, not to mention self-pity and self-condemnation. Unhealthy blame provides the excuse for not accepting the responsibility to change.

Recognition

I stopped blaming my dad for our one-way relationship the day after I visited him with my friend Michael. That previous day had been highlighted by the drive to visit him after we had had no contact for several months. He acted cold, distant, and unconcerned. I felt wounded and offended once again, especially because it happened in the presence of my friend. Michael tried his best to carry on a conversation by asking questions about my childhood. My dad gave token answers and turned aside. When I left I silently vowed not to put myself in that embarrassing position again. I had had enough! I drove home, disturbed and angry. I was very upset. The embarrassment added to my pain. That evening I shared my anger and frustration with my wife. She told me to pray and forgive him. I didn't want to—I was tired of forgiving him. Reluctantly I agreed and went outside. I spent some time thinking, and finally I prayed. This time it was different. In my prayer I shared my deepest feelings about the relationship. My self-doubts. My anger. My hurt. My fears. Finally tears of relief came and I walked back into the house. I awoke the next morning with a new thought: "I am in a one-way relationship with my dad, and it's not going to change." My prayer the night before had brought God's revelation.

I realized the truth about how we relate to each other as I never had before. Every time I reach out, he responds. If I don't reach out, he won't respond. If I remain absent for long, he's negative and rejecting, but if I maintain routine contact, he's friendly. I was taking the major responsibility for maintaining the relationship. It wasn't an issue of his not caring for me, but rather a situation where the caring was on one-way terms. And those terms involved little risk on his part. That was why he wouldn't come to my house for family dinners or reach out in other ways. That is also why I was so offended. I wanted the relationship on *my* terms, not his. I was the one who had to reach out, or the relationship would not work. I would much rather have had it the other way. I was jealous that he had his way so easily.

It had taken years for me to see this pattern of one-sidedness. I always knew something was wrong but couldn't see that I did not have to carry guilt for the relationship's not working. Recognition opened the path to change. We can't be healed when we lack awareness of what the true problem is and why it is there. Knowledge of the real problem cleared away the confusion. It allowed me to focus. I was able to direct my energy and prayer into facing and resolving the problem. But there was a price to pay. A part of me didn't really want to face the truth. Sometimes it is easier to deny the severity of the problem rather than to look deeply inside and discover the ugly or painful parts. It hurts to face something painful, but it hurts more not to. The truth hurts, but it will set you free. Denial soothes our senses but keeps us in bondage.

As I faced the truth of a one-way relationship, I had to deal rightly with the blame. I couldn't just blame him or myself and leave things at that. I now had to accept the responsibility to change. My priority shifted from how to resolve things with my dad to how to resolve my own hurt, resentment, and jealousy issues. I had done inner examinations before but not with this clarity of focus. This was the painful part. I could no longer honestly say the problem was with my dad only. I truly began to see how I was part of the problem. I was longing to be loved. I was caring in order to be cared for. I was giving to get. Too much of what I did was for the wrong reason.

My challenge was to understand my own self-defeating attitudes of loving, caring, and pleasing. I needed to find a release from the power these emotions had over my life. My focus was no longer on how to fix the relationship with my dad but rather on how to fix me. This step was the hardest but also the healthiest.

Ownership

Recognition is difficult because it requires ownership. It requires us to accept our responsibility in the problem. It is much easier to blame the other person than it is to face the truth about ourselves. It is much easier to see the weaknesses in everyone else and ignore the sin in our own life. It is also easier to slip into self-pity and self-judgment instead of courageous self-appraisal. I needed to see what in me wanted and even demanded a relationship that the other person did not want equally.

I needed to realize I wasn't just a victim of my dad's one-sidedness.

Does this mean there are no such things as victims? No. There are true victims. Kids are usually true victims of their parents and other authority figures. Kids have no power or ability to act independently. There are also rape and assault victims who had no complicity or power to resist.

But adults in one-way relationships are not powerless to act. Even the wife of an abusive husband needs to see her complicity in allowing the abuse to continue. She is not responsible for the abuse, but she is responsible for her reactions to it.

Adopting the identity of victim is both self-defeating and dangerous. It can cause us to continue being victimized by our own lack of responsibility. It also causes us to misuse our gifts, talents, and energies.

This is how Julia described her victimization:

Victimized by Me

You know a habit is ingrained when you find yourself thinking, *But doesn't everybody do it this way?* I have been exposed to the concept of victims for a while now. One of the first things I learned was that there really is no such role in God's economy.

That stunned me. If I couldn't be the victim, who would I be? What role would I play? The shock eventually wore off and I reverted to my old habits, unchanged. However, like any good teacher of slow children, God uses repetition. So here I am again, having to face myself as the victim. (Did you catch that "have to" phrase? I'm doing it again.)

As a victim I never just did things. I *had* to do them. I was forced to do them by "people, places, things, and God," especially God. P.P.T. and G. also prevented me from doing things. No matter how badly I wanted to, I couldn't, thanks to either P.P.T. or G.

There was the time I decided that I didn't want to go to hell so I *had* to accept Christ. Or the time I wanted to go to college but *had* to stay home with the kids instead. I also *had* to reconcile my relationship with my parents. I *had* to work out conflicts with my husband. Finally, I *had* to get help with my weight problem.

Oddly enough, all these decisions were to my benefit. Every one made my life better. Yet I continually find myself thinking in a style reminiscent of my six-year-old: "Ick, I *have* to do *all* the housework."

It's no wonder I have a problem with resentment, with this mind set. I have seen myself as being forced all my life. Nor is it a surprise that I have problems relating to God. He has been the head bad guy forcing me to do all these uncomfortable things.

So where's the payoff? What's in this victim mode for me? My reward for being the victim is to escape from responsibility. They made me do it. Or they wouldn't let me do it. Either way, it's not my fault.

This style may be okay for kids. No doubt it appealed to me as a kid. For an adult, however, it stinks. I mentioned the resentment and estrangement from God that it causes. Added to that is the strain of manipulating P.P.T. and G. into forcing me to do what I really wanted to do in the first place.

A case in point is the turmoil I have encountered regarding our pending move to a small town. I can't find a single circumstance that forces me to make the move. Even God seems to be saying that I can go or stay. So what do I do now? A lifetime of reacting does not prepare one for taking action. I find it infinitely hard to simply say, "I want to move; therefore, with God's permission, I will."

Fear gnaws at me. What if we make a mistake? What if we haven't really heard from God? What if we find out that we really don't like small towns?

Friends to whom I can hardly relate say things like "So what if you do make a mistake? Can't God use mistakes? How else will you learn to hear from God if you don't try it out?"

Yes, God can use mistakes but I am reluctant to go through all that effort just to learn. I'd rather take a class or listen to a sermon. Walking through a lesson does not appeal to me at all.

So the bottom line is that I choose to be a victim because

it is easy and it absolves me of responsibility. Too bad it doesn't work. The price of avoiding paying the price of maturing is getting higher every day. My strength budget is definitely limited, so today I think I'll eliminate the middleman of avoidance and go straight for wholesale maturity.

By the grace of God, I will no longer be the victim of anyone or anything. Rather, I'll take an active role. I've put on my walking shoes, so bring on the lessons!

Good-bye Victim!
Hello Disciple!

As Julia has learned, it is not healthy to assume the role or identity of a victim. Neither is it healthy to try to blame one or the other person for a relationship pattern that doesn't work. It is much healthier to look for what each does to contribute to the problem. And it's healthier yet to be more concerned with our responsibility to change than with the other person's. *Facing ourselves does not mean we take total responsibility for a failing relationship. Rather it means we take total responsibility for ourselves in the relationship.* It means examining not only what we do but why we do it. This is our only guarantee of not being a hypocrite. It is also our only hope for change.

We cannot change others. How long have you tried to change them or waited for them to change and seen it not work? But we can change ourselves through rigorous honesty and God's power. We are not to blame for the relationship. We give ourselves too much credit.

Loving, caring, or giving too much for the wrong reasons is the issue we need to resolve within ourselves. It is a reflection of a need for change in us, not just an indication of an unhealthy relationship. If we blame another for all the relationship problems, nothing will change. If we condemn ourselves for all the problems, nothing will change.

But if we use the relationship problem as an opportunity to see the things in us that need healing and change, then we and the relationship can change. Blame of others or self can be a trap for not taking the responsibility to change. The wrong question to ask is "Who's to blame?" The right question is "What is this relationship showing me about my need to change?"

Chapter 3

The "other" person in a one-way
relationship often needs
less of our brand of love
and more of our honesty,
less pampering, and
more accountability.

3 How to Deal with the Other Person in a One-Way Relationship

HOW SHOULD WE VIEW the other person in our one-way relationship—as life's winners or losers? To be pitied or praised? Sally, like most people in one-way relationships, had strong feelings about her one-way partner.

"This is unfair. He was always the lucky one who got everything his own way. I tried to be everything he needed, and it still didn't work. Why can't someone be devoted to me for a change?"

She felt like a loser and believed him to be the winner. She wished she could be the lucky one who gets all the needed love and has everything her way, the one who doesn't have to give the most. In essence, Sally was saying she no longer wished to be the one who gave too much; she preferred to be the object of someone else's giving too much.

I am convinced a great many of us have secretly desired this. Everyone to some degree, especially those of us who love, care, or give too much, desire someone else's total devotion to us. We are somewhat jealous of the other person. We want not only the love we never received or lost but added love to make up for all the lack. This is what we are desperately striving to find. But is this really good for us? Is this really what we need?

I don't think so. I have concluded that it would not be good to swap places with the person on the receiving end of a one-way relationship. Being cared for and loved more than we return is rarely good for us. The one who gives less becomes less—less giving, less caring, less focused on God and others. One becomes more self-centered and unfulfilled. Needs that are pampered and fed bring greater appetites, not lesser ones. Too much love and care is as deadly as too little. It takes more and more love and care to feel loved and cared for. Soon the expectation is set that others owe us love, care, and assistance. Our focus becomes self-oriented, we can't see beyond our own needs, and the expectations of others elude us.

People don't really profit from being loved too much. A test of true and healthy love is its effect on the person being loved. True love seeks the best for the beloved. Did your love or care and giving create a greater love, result in kinder actions or more responsibility being assumed? Or did it help breed self-centeredness and irresponsibility? We need to examine if our love or care has really diminished the other person—how our love or care or giving has resulted in one who is less loving, less responsible, less caring, and more self-centered. We have become part of the other's problem by encouraging the weakness of not mutually sharing love and becoming vulnerable. This analysis is a very difficult step because it will not always be clear how our actions have affected the other. It is a step that usually requires counsel and advice. We need to ask what is perceived in us that seems to be contributing to the problem, not only in ourselves but in the other person's life.

Sally cared for others in such a way that it often cost the recipient more than was gained. She shined her husband's shoes, fixed his breakfast, woke him up on time. When he rose in the morning, his clothes were laid out for him. Everything was done for him. She did too much; he did too little. He became less responsible and less of a person because of it. The technical word for this is "enabling," which in this context means to assist someone wrongly. To enable is to take a responsibility that someone should be assuming alone. To enable is to assume a responsibility that God never gave us for the person's life. When accountability for another is taken over, both the enabler and the other person become less. Responsibilities that are not ours but that we take anyway will often curse, not bless, us.

Betty's overresponsibility for her grown daughter jeopardized her own health. Her doctor warned that it might cost her life because of the stress it put on her heart and her overall physical condition.

If We Let Go, God Will Pick Up

Examine how your love might be enabling the other person. Are you doing too much? Are you making alibis or excuses for irresponsible behavior? What about overprotectiveness? Are you afraid of not doing enough and is that fear motivating your overgiving?

I have learned through many years that if we let go, God will pick up. People, especially our mates and adult children, belong to God, not us. Only in rare circumstances may we take significant responsibility for the life and welfare of another adult.

Too many one-way relationships of caring, giving, or loving weaken the other person's character. The dictionary defines character as moral and ethical strength. Pampering another's needs weakens the desire and ability to do what is right. We need love, care, and concern balanced with challenge, sacrifice, and difficulty. "As iron sharpens iron, so does one man's countenance sharpen another," the Scripture says. A healthy relationship has a certain amount of sharpening to it as we react to one another. In a healthy relationship not only do we love and care, but we also challenge and strengthen. The relationship makes us more than our self-centeredness would like us to be. Being on the receiving end of a one-way relationship takes away the challenge. It takes off the edge of pressure that makes us grow. The ones who love less become less. There is a danger in being jealous of the other person. We become more self-centered, too self-focused; we want to take care of ourselves too much and want others to love us too much. We give up our obligation to love rightly.

Some don't really want to trade places—we'd rather fix the other person instead. This is especially true of the spouses of addicted people and the parents of troubled kids. We feel sorry for the other person and want to do something to help. We see the person as troubled; we know there are problems, wounds, or rejections that have never been healed. We feel a need to fix those problems in order to make the hurt go away—to put an end to suffering and failure.

My always-nice friend brought home every stray cat and dog she found. She even brought home street people and fed them. She couldn't stand seeing someone hurt. This only made her husband angry, but she couldn't stop doing it. She knew what it was like not to have love in her life. Loving the strays was a replacement for loving herself. She gave to them the love she needed. She felt for them because she felt for herself.

There's also another way we can feel for ourselves while thinking we are caring for others. We try to prevent the failures of our children or loved ones in order to preserve our reputation or assuage our guilt.

Betty's worry about what her friends would think if her daughter had one more failed marriage made her fearful and drove her to try to fix the situation. Parents frequently bail their children out of bad financial situations or buy them gifts to feel less guilty about not giving them emotionally healthy love, care, or concern.

This type of loving, caring, giving, or feeling too much is really a self-love. While it makes us feel better about ourselves if we can help alleviate the pain, it is, in truth, really our own unrecognized and unresolved pain that causes us to over-identify. Rarely working well, this kind of loving, caring, or giving doesn't resolve anyone's problems.

The other person in a one-way relationship is usually wounded. Having made an inner decision not to love, care, or be responsible, the person puts up a shield of invulnerability, promising to give only in certain ways, at certain times, pledging never to risk total giving, thus covertly avoiding responsibility. Until those inner decisions or vows are challenged and changed, our way of loving, caring, or giving will not effect change or resolve our pain. Even though it may offer some momentary influence, it is not a cure.

This, in part, answers the question of what to do with the other person, who usually needs less of our brand of love and more of our honesty, less pampering and more accountability. Our partner in the one-way relationship needs to understand that we also are wounded and weak, that we all carry our own wounds and troubles in life. The individual who is unwilling to face those wounds and weaknesses and offer them for healing will never be healthy in a relationship. The most difficult person to counsel is the one who does not want to look inside. The most difficult person to love is the one who does not want to be vulnerable, the one who does not want to face the humanity within us all. For these people, change isn't likely. Scott Peck has named them "people of the lie," the lie being the belief that change is unnecessary.

When the other person in a one-way relationship cannot see the need for change, we will continue to be victimized and be used. In powerful one-way relationships the other person will also become abusive. If physical abuse is already present, get help immediately. Don't put yourself or your loved ones in physical danger. Act immediately. The situation will not improve without the help of someone else.

What should you do if you find yourself emotionally abused, victimized, or wounded by others? Should you excuse the sin against you and continue in the relationship? Should you detach, separate, divorce? Being abandoned or abused—which is the worse pain? Is there some other answer?

These are hard questions to answer, and each person's situation needs to be carefully examined. What is right for one may not be perfectly right for the other. The wise counsel of a pastor or professional is usually needed. Don't, however, continue in the fantasy that your unconditional love or protection can make the situation better. If that were true, your repeated attempts would already have worked!

Unconditional love with no strings attached can sometimes help convince the other party that it is safe to look inside, that there will be someone who will care and help with the healing. But it is rare that the unconditional love can come from us in such a way that it can be received. It takes God and His unconditional love to bring someone to the place of trusting, to cause the heart to break open and be guided to vulnerability and willingness to change.

The other person in a one-way relationship also needs to face inner hurt and self as we are having to face ours. This is the only hope for change. And our only hope for change is first to face ourselves before facing another. The Scripture says to take the beam out of our own eye before we remove the speck out of the other person's eye lest we be called hypocrites. Focusing first on our own contribution to the pattern is our only assurance of clear eyesight and right motive. As each of us faces our own wrong motives of jealousy and self-love, we will be better able to deal with the other person and the unhealthy one-way patterns. We need to refocus on ourselves in a healthy way.

Learn how to be honest with yourself and others. Seek God for the deep healing you need. Let Him take control of your life and needs. Don't detach and run away. Don't use another person as the standard of what's right and healthy. Don't become preoccupied with others, envying their place. Instead, concentrate your efforts on facing your own need for change. One-way relationships don't get fixed by our changing the other person or getting rid of the relationship. Our society has tried that. Witness the immense number of second and third marriages and the relationships that still fail. We've been changing partners instead of changing ourselves. This has caused us to repeat mistakes by selecting other nonrisking, relationally dysfunctional people. Then we wonder why the relationship doesn't work.

The only part of the one-way relationship problem we can fix is us. The other person needs healing and change. The other person needs accountability, not our bitterness, which only makes it more difficult for him or her to face the problem. Our anger and judgment aren't needed. They only reinforce a protective desire. Our rejection just verifies underlying suspicions. What is needed are our prayers, our honesty, and, where appropriate, our unconditional love.

The other person in a one-way relationship is a wounded, damaged person who will continue to be less until able to love more. Intimacy and love in a relationship can be healing, but they must be mutual to be beneficial.

The problem with one-way relationships is the sickness of spirit they create in us all. We love in order to be loved or give in order to avoid pain. Again the other person gives less and becomes less. Both of us are deficient in our loving. Sacrificial love is still the standard of the universe, and it entails giving. You can't love without giving even though you can give without loving. The motive behind the giving reveals the truth. We need to see that people who love too much are wanting too much to be loved. People who don't love enough are also bound by their self-love. The hope for one-way relationships is the healing that God can bring to the deep need for love in both of us. This only comes as we see the truth about ourselves and our relationships. The first step toward change is seeing how we have contributed to the one-way relationship problem through our own jealousies and self-love and accepting our responsibility to change.

A friend once said, "Fill up your inner cup of needs with God, and then when you add people, places, things, or disappointments, it still will overflow. Doing it the other way will always drain your cup, not fill it." We have tried too hard to fill our deep inner cup of needs with people first rather than with God. The effort has drained us instead of fulfilling us. For most of us it has become what and who we are. It is a style of relating ingrained at birth and reinforced throughout life. But it is changeable for those of us who have the courage to face ourselves and God, the God who said, "I have loved you with an everlasting love. Therefore I have drawn you with loving kindness. . . . I know the plans that I have for you, . . . plans for welfare and not for calamity, to give you a future and a hope" (Jer. 31:3; 29:11 (NASB)).

Chapter 4

The tendency toward
codependency is in us all.
We love, care, and give
in a relationship for
the wrong reasons. It has
become a style of relating
ingrained at birth and
reinforced throughout life.

4   Introducing Codependency: The New Term for the Root Problem in Relationships

IT'S A NEW INSIGHT into the old problem of loving, caring, or giving too much for the wrong reasons. Codependency has become a buzzword in the self-help and professional counseling fields. It's discussed on all the talk shows and is one of the main reasons I've written this book. There is a lot of confusion. Definitions of codependency range from a personality disorder, a disease, to just a negative trait. Any of these may be true, depending on how powerful it is in your life.

Codependency is the tendency in all of us to love, care, or give in a relationship for the wrong reasons. Codependency is what one-way relationships are all about. It's the professional term for the desperate need in all of us:

- to love in order to be loved
- to give in order to get
- to care in order to be cared for
- to please in order to be accepted
- to pamper and placate in order to avoid consequences

Codependency

Codependency is a problem in us that doesn't get fixed by changing the other person or dissolving the relationship.

Our society has tried that. Witness the high percentage of second and third marriages and relationships that don't work. Codependents have been changing partners instead of changing themselves, which in turn causes repeated relationship mistakes by selecting other nongiving, relationally dysfunctional people. Then they wonder why the relationship doesn't work. *For most of us, codependency has become a style of relating ingrained at birth and reinforced throughout life.*

Codependency is of epidemic proportions in our culture. It is not found in all relationships, but it is apparent in most. Rarely does a person love, care, or give sacrificially, expecting nothing in return. Most of us have some pattern or flavor of codependency in our relationships. Some are profoundly one-way and powerfully codependent while others may have only a flavor or hint of one-sidedness. Codependency is not an all-or-nothing situation. It is a matter of degree. Many relationships have unhealthy patterns of codependency right along with the healthy ones. The codependent patterns, when left unresolved, sour the healthy love, care, and concern.

The concept of codependency was born out of the extensive work with alcoholics and their spouses. The alcoholic was the dependent because of the addiction to alcohol. The spouse of the alcoholic came to be called the codependent, also trapped in the dependence of the spouse. As therapists worked with these families, it became apparent the majority were in a one-way relationship with the addict, giving, caring, loving, going the extra mile to try to halt the drinking. All the while, the alcoholic would progressively become more abusive or withdrawn. The more the spouse sacrificed, the more the alcoholic indulged. When one became more irresponsible, the other took on more responsibility. It was like a balancing act. The more one did, the less the other cared. The loving, caring, and giving made things worse, not better. The pattern was well established and well known in alcohol addiction treatment circles but nowhere else.

As addiction therapists began working with more alcoholic families, they soon saw the same one-way patterns in other relationships and marriages. This gave rise to the now-popular concept of codependence in relationships. Codependence is only a new name for an old problem. The human race has always had difficulty with wrong patterns of loving, caring, or giving. We have always had difficulty learning how to love in a healthy way. Many facets of our culture reflect this problem. Country music songs are well known for lamenting one-way loving and broken hearts. *Gone with the Wind* and other classic movies of the forties and fifties powerfully dramatized one-way loving. Literary classics have spoken for centuries to the issue of unrequited love and its tragic results. These are all codependency issues.

Why We Love, Care, and Give

This tendency in all of us to love for the wrong reasons, especially evident in one-way relationships, is also the driving force behind most relationship problems. It addresses the very issue of why we love, care, and give. Codependency creates difficulty for us in four crucial areas of life:

Needs

Our need for others to love, care for, appreciate, admire, or listen to us can become overly important. Our need to avoid pain can become an obsession. We may want these needs met too much. The need can begin to control us without our realizing it, and we end up frustrated or tormented because it doesn't happen. Sally became tormented by her need to have her husbands' approval and love. She used to beg Phil not to be angry with her, and she continued to polish Bob's shoes in the hope that he would appreciate her and pay attention to her. Her need for them to love her became so powerful that it controlled her, and she was powerless to prevent it.

Power

The other person's wants, needs, or expectations can

end up having more power and control over us than our own conscience or desires. We can become preoccupied with what someone else wants or needs in order to lead a healthy, fruitful life. Betty was caught up this way in her daughter's life. She second-guessed the younger woman's every move and wondered what she was thinking. She went out of her way to do things for her daughter that were not appreciated or wanted. Whatever we think the most about and give priority credence to is what has the power over our lives. Betty's daughter inadvertently controlled Betty's life, having more power over Betty than she had over herself.

Emotions

Fear, anger, hurt, pain, guilt, disappointment, or anxiety can begin to dominate our lives. The emotions end up ruling. We are often out of control and wonder why since "they" are the problem. Sally was tremendously upset by Bob's leaving, but at the same time there was a strange sense of relief in all this, a relief from the torment she had felt. Her emotions had gotten out of control. She had been constantly fearful that she was doing the wrong thing. The torment and insecurity that he would not care for her or love her and that he would be angry and disapprove of her ruled her life. Those emotions had more control than she had over herself.

Reactions

We can establish a pattern of reacting rather than responding. The other person's actions or failure to act can control us by triggering an immediate reaction. For some the reaction is outward and evident. For others it is silent, deep, and hidden. But it is always there. My nice friend's heart would pound fast, and she could feel the anxiety rise up the back of her neck every time her husband looked at her out of the corner of his eye. She was afraid he would be disappointed or angry with her. No one around her saw the reaction, but she felt it and, as a result, would redouble her efforts to make sure that she was nice and did not do anything wrong. Her automatic reactions controlled her. She was not able to control them.

In codependency we are so dependent on the other person and what we want from him or her that we are not in control of ourselves. We have put our trust in people, places, and things, looking to these to meet deep inner needs, needs that can be met only by a living God. Our love has become too enmeshed with our need to be loved and to protect ourselves from pain. Our attempt to fulfill our innermost desires and heal our wounds is not working. Other people are controlling our lives. The need for their love, attention, or well-being is controlling. They have become our God.

Healing codependency is difficult because it requires ownership. It requires us to admit our own responsibility in the problem. Ownership is an essential step to healing anything within us. It is much easier to blame another person than it is to face the truth about ourselves. It is more comfortable to see the weaknesses in everyone else rather than the sin in our own lives. I needed to see what was in me that wanted, even demanded, a relationship with my dad, a need to which he was obviously impervious. One-way relationships and codependent relationships can be deceiving. It is not always immediately clear how much responsibility to take or how much blame to give. The only assurance we have of being able to deal rightly with the other person is to take ownership and responsibility for our part in the right spirit by seeing how we contribute to the problem.

Codependents need to face the fact of their codependency. That means that there is something in us that needs to change first before we can concern ourselves with the other person. This was the painful part for me. I could no longer honestly say the problem was with my dad. I began to see how I was loving to be loved, how I was caring in order to be cared for, how I was giving to get. My priority shifted from how to resolve things with my dad to how to resolve issues within me. I had done inner examinations before but not with this clarity of focus. My challenge was to understand my own self-defeating attitudes of loving, caring, and pleasing. I needed to find a release from the dominating power those attitudes had over my life. My focus shifted from what was wrong with my dad to how to restore me.

In most instances there is a payoff to not facing ourselves. Sally liked to dress well. Every rejection by her husband spurred her to go on a shopping spree to assuage the hurt and act out her bitterness. Her shopping sprees were an extravagant way of comforting herself and punishing him at the same time. In codependency there are also payoffs. Before blaming the other person, ask yourself what benefit you are receiving from continuing to be codependent. What is your response to the lack of care, concern, or love you feel? Careful self-analysis is your only guarantee against being a hypocrite.

Examine the following relationship characteristics. They are all symptoms of one-way codependency. They will help you recognize the truth and take ownership of your codependency. The more characteristics you match, the more codependent your relationship is likely to be.

- Do you consistently love, care, give, or take more responsibility than the other person?
- Do you "tiptoe" around the person for fear of what may be said, done, or felt?
- Do you have difficulty being totally honest, direct, and loving in your communication with the person?
- Do you spend time second-guessing another's motives, needs, or actions?
- Do you cover, lie, alibi, excuse, or justify others' behavior to yourself or someone else?
- Do you find yourself being regularly critical, blaming, or negative about or toward the person?
- Do you feel the need to fix the person or to convince the person that you're right and he or she is wrong?
- Do you constantly feel the need to give in or give up just to keep the peace?

- Do you have trouble maintaining a steady emotional life when another person goes up or down?
- Do you worry, obsess, or become tormented about that person or your relationship?
- Are you the one who must always first admit you're wrong and apologize or beg in order to resolve conflicts?
- Are you the one who always has to go the extra mile to make the relationship work?

My one-sided relationship with my dad possessed a number of these characteristics. I took the major responsibility to make our relationship work. I went the extra mile. I also tiptoed around him and tried to please by saying and doing only things which met with his approval. I made excuses to my kids for him when he didn't show up for dinners or didn't send Christmas presents. I shared accomplishments and made small talk but left out the weightier issues of heart and life. It made for a superficial and at times awkward circumstance for both of us. I wasn't honest and direct. When he didn't reciprocate, I became hurt and angry and gave up only to change my mind later and try again. The pattern didn't change until the day I surrendered in prayer. My resignation led to God's revelation. The awareness of being in a one-way relationship brought my codependency to light. I began to examine the issue of one-sidedness. How long had the relationship been that way? Where did the one-sidedness come from? Am I trapped in this same pattern with others? Are there parts of this I'm not seeing? More thought and better clarity came from my digging.

What You Can Do

But what do you do once the codependency is revealed in yourself or others? Do you condemn yourself or the other person or detach and distance yourself from the relationship or demand change? Codependents are not evil people.

Rather, they are wounded individuals who require honest and loving reactions to their needs. The awareness of co-dependency in a marriage or any relationship can spark greater problems if it is not dealt with carefully. This letter vividly expresses that difficulty. See what happened in this couple's marriage.

Dear Mr. Ells,

I am writing this letter to express my concern regarding the teaching of codependency. Although I do believe that it is an important issue, I strongly feel it must be taught with balance at all times. Both my wife and I realized that we had areas in our lives that were codependent. My wife then purchased a secular book on codependency, read it, and came to the conclusion that I was very codependent on her. During this time I started facing some very deep struggles in my walk with God, my position at work, and my marriage. I had really been hurting badly for the last nine months, and I was crying out to God for help and healing. The loneliness started becoming unbearable—there was no answer from God, no peace at work, and no peace at home. I could have really used some encouragement and caring from my wife, but she didn't know how to do that anymore—she was too afraid of making me more codependent. I couldn't find my way out of the desperate situation for a long time. Only God's grace spared me. God has answered my cries, but the pain, hurt, and mistrust are now difficult issues to deal with. It seems that although the codependency teaching can bring freedom to individuals, it has the potential of severely damaging a marriage by taking a union which God intended to be as "one flesh" and making a marriage of two independent people, both afraid of codependency—so afraid that the love and compassion that are required for a healthy marriage are destroyed because of misunderstanding. . . . I pray that you will seek God concerning a balanced presentation of codependency. I am praying for you.

In this relationship the wife recognized her husband's codependency and detached herself from her normal pattern of care, love, and concern. It came at a difficult time in his life and wounded him deeply. It has also caused him concern over what a biblically balanced presentation of codependency should be.

This reaction is not uncommon. The current teaching on this subject has created much confusion and reactiveness. What should she have done when she saw his codependency? What should he do with his? Does the recognition of codependency require one to give less love, care, and compassion in a marriage? Does the recognition of codependency have the potential of severely damaging the "one flesh" marriage God has ordained?

These are all honest questions, each one needing an answer. Codependency is a wrong way of relating. We need to deal with it as we would deal with any discovered pattern of unhealthiness. Definitions are abundant. Resolution comes slowly.

Do Not Panic

Realize you are in the same boat as countless others. There is no such thing as a perfect marriage or relationship having no codependent patterns. All of us fall short, and each of us could and should grow more healthy in relationships. Some relationships are severely one-way and codependent; others, only mildly so. Yours is not some unusual problem that no one else has to cope with. We all struggle with learning how to love, care, and give rightly. Maybe you are having more difficulty, but you are not alone.

Set Your Heart on Healthiness, Not Perfection

Maybe you are stuck at the same place Sally was when she asked me during a counseling session, "How can a marriage be healthy when it has problems?" She had been to a Christian self-help group called New Wine. Someone in her discussion group had shared about a relationship which was becoming healthy even though there were codependency issues. A relationship does not need to be perfectly mutual or noncodependent to be healthy. Health is different from perfection. Health is an honest recognition of our need to change and a fearless commitment to change in God's way. We become healthy when we're rigorously honest with ourselves and others about ourselves and our relationship. There is healthiness in the man who wrote the letter. He is being honest with himself, God, and others about his struggle. He will find an answer to his codependency and marriage. He may have to deal with a lot of pain on the way, but he will get there and the pain will ease. His honesty is the quality that will allow him to be healthy in an imperfect relationship and change. Honesty, however, is hard to come by for most. It requires the risk of being viewed as wrong. No one likes being wrong; we all want to be right. But accepting our wrongness is essential to change. New-Age philosophy encourages us to view right and wrong according to our perception rather than from a healthy, biblical perspective. Change entails the risk of rejection. Revealing our inner selves to others creates the feeling of vulnerability and the risk of being wounded by rejection. Pain and shame from the past must be overcome before we can be honest enough to become healthy.

Learn the Right Thing to Do

Later in this book you will have a reference base for what is healthy and right. It gives you a goal to aim for and a benchmark for evaluating your circumstance. Many codependents are not really sure of what to aim for. They know only that they want what they do not have. Be aware of the roles and rules of a healthy relationship.

Do not make your primary goal simply stopping all codependent behavior. That is too negative and reactive in focus. Instead, make your goal one of seeking how God wants your relationship to work. Introducing this understanding will have the benefit of reducing confusion and reactiveness while still promoting change. Other chapters describe a healthy, biblical understanding of marriage and relationships. Prayerfully studied steps of what it takes to make a relationship healthy will guide you as you begin your change.

Seek Help

Few codependent patterns can be rightly worked out without help from someone else. A Christian counselor, experienced pastor, or healthy support group is important. We are seldom objective enough to reveal our own ingrained patterns truthfully. Someone else's objectivity will keep us on track. It will also assist us in dealing rightly and fairly with the other person. My wife provided the balance and input I needed to deal rightly in the relationship with my dad.

Inviting another person into your life will also provide accountability. It will help you do what you say you are committed to doing. Accountability will help you change. Be careful where you seek help. Friends or others who make you feel supported but do not require you to acknowledge your contribution to the problem are not a solution. We all need to see our weakness and sin in order to change. Hand-holding is insufficient.

If You Are Willing, Trust God to Be Able

The basic issue of change has to be your willingness, not your ability. Few of us have the power to change our lives. We do, however, gain the ability to choose change by facing our fears and hurt. God has the power to change us if we are willing to ask and seek diligently. It is usually our fear and self-love that keep us from changing. We are afraid of what will happen to us if we stop doing it our way and let God do it His way. My old ways of relating may not work, but they are still comfortable and familiar. The unknown is frightening. But if we are willing to trust, then we will change. Prayer and the surrender of our will to God are the essential beginning ingredients of change.

Codependency is a relational addiction. The unhealed wounds and unresolved losses cause us to do things to please ourselves and others rather than God. People, places, and things become too important in our lives. We try to fulfill deep inner needs through relationships that are not working. The answer is to fill the deep inner spaces with God instead of people. As we invite Jesus deeper into the recesses of our hearts and pain, He becomes more real to us. He soon becomes our inner strength and support. We do not need others as desperately. We do not need their love, approval, or attention as much. When Jesus fills our inner being, people, places, and things will not control our lives. Instead they will fill our lives in a satisfying way.

God is the answer to all deep needs, especially relationship needs. The empowerment for each step in the healing process comes from God. Each of the healing steps requires deep self-examination, and each also requires God's help. Coming to know one's weaknesses, pains, and problems is of no great value in and of itself. It can only make you a more enlightened miserable person. The goal of self-discovery is healing, not awareness or intellectual understanding.

Many are not healed because they cannot trust. Trust is a key issue. We need to trust in a power greater than ourselves to deliver us from our codependency. Jesus has the power to heal; we do not. We need to trust in His willingness and ability to heal the codependency in our lives; thus we can learn to be controlled by inner sources rather than outward circumstances.

Chapter 5

Codependency is
a wounded heart's
cry for love.

5 | Why Are Codependents Codependent?

IN ADDRESSING THIS QUESTION I feel the way William Tell must have felt while he shot the apple off his son's head. If he hit the target, everyone would applaud. If not, he has not only failed but made everything worse by shooting his own son.

As every codependent becomes more aware, a question comes to light: "Why am I this way?"

In reading different books, you'll see a lot of reasons given for codependency:

"Codependents can't set boundaries."

"They can't take care of themselves."

"They came from a dysfunctional family."

"They are trying to get the love they never got."

"They've been victimized and wounded."

I believe all these reasons are true, but I feel most lack depth in explaining why a codependent becomes that way. The "why" starts with an understanding of how codependency results from violating the universal laws of love.

We readily accept the existence of physical laws in nature. The law of gravity accurately predicts that if I walk off the end of a roof I will fall and be hurt. We learned this law of physics at a young age. And we try to abide by it. There are also, however, psychosocial laws that govern our relationships, the most crucial ones being the universal laws of love. These also have predictive value. If we violate them, there are enduring natural consequences to cause us hurt or pain.

Codependents are everywhere. They illustrate that at

the very heart of loving, caring, or giving too much for the wrong reason is the inability to care for one's self in a healthy manner. This incapacity is tied, in turn, to the codependent's inability to care for others in a healthy manner. As so many others have written, the ability to love others rightly is directly related to how we love ourself. Thus, the second law of love states, "Love your neighbor as yourself."

Codependents do not love their "neighbor" the same way they love themselves. They love as they would like to be loved in return. They secretly desire their neighbor to love them as they love the neighbor. What they want is what they give. What they give is what they want—what they are unable to provide themselves.

Codependents have a damaged ability to love, care, or give because they somehow have never been able to resolve their own issues of self-love.

This makes the root reasons for codependency deeply personal, obviously relational, and necessarily spiritual. Codependents do not fully accept themselves. They have a difficult time loving others in the right way and need the deep inner love and peace only a spiritual awakening can bring.

Resolving Codependency

Codependents are codependent because they have not come to peace with themselves, God, and others. Many inner needs are still not fully met, too many wounds are not healed, and losses are unresolved. Codependents have unfinished business deep within about God and others, about love and life. They need to take responsibility for fulfilling their own personal needs, learning how God does this, while appropriating His strength to do it.

To resolve codependency fully will require facing the enemy within and overcoming its effect in their lives. Carl Jung wrote:

> In actual life it requires the greatest discipline to be simple, and the acceptance of oneself is the essence of the moral

problem and the epitome of a whole outlook upon life. That I feed the hungry and that I forgive an insult and that I love my enemy in the name of Christ. All these are undoubtedly great virtues. What I do unto the least of my brethren, that I do unto Christ.

But what if I should discover that the least among them all, the poorest of all the beggars, the most impudent of all the offenders and the very enemy himself; that these are within me? And that I myself am the enemy who must be loved? What then? As a rule, the Christian's attitude is then reversed. There is no longer any question of love or long-suffering. We say to the brother within us, *Raca! You fool,* and we condemn and rage against ourselves, and then we hide it from the world. We refuse to admit ever having met this least among the lowly in ourselves.

Codependents have an enemy within, a deep inner voice of rage, rejection, shame, or pain that prohibits them being at peace. This voice drives us to give others the love, care, or attention we need. It also keeps us from being honest with ourselves or others about who we really are. For to be truly known, we must be known by God.

I have had trouble in each of these areas. I've had an enemy within that has fueled my codependency since childhood. It has been a nagging inner voice and feeling of insecurity, inferiority, and self-doubt. It is very difficult to live with those feelings of inadequacy. The feeling is so painful that we will try almost anything to alleviate it. We will especially do things to please, impress, or even convince others of how great we are so that they will love us. This is the motive behind the one who acts the part of the "bigshot," who is trying to win the inner battle by gathering admiration. We will love, care, or give to have those emotions returned. The love and care from others helps to fight the enemy within.

This becomes the source of our many manipulations and defenses in life as we manipulate others to give us the love and affection we so desperately need. We also defend against the truth others may share regarding our weaknesses because it feeds the internal enemy. We are always trying to win the battle.

In little girls this sometimes gets translated into seductivity. Sally was an example of this. So was my always-nice friend. Seductivity is a quality of attractiveness a person develops to purposely get needed attention, affection, or affirmation. This quality can be expressed through dress, even to the point of wearing revealing attire. Or it can be manifested in dressing neatly as a pin in the latest fashion. Each can be a calculated attempt to attract seductively.

Teenage girls learn how to be seductive through dress and flirtation. Some seductiveness is cultural and not a concern. But much of it is really an indication of a wounded heart's cry for love, a wounded child's attempt to overcome the undiscovered enemy within.

This is why some women become promiscuous, why they give sex to get love. They are purposely trying to appeal to a man's or boy's sexual nature in order to get the needed attention.

The recent hard-body craze is an attempt to have a good outer image so that the inner battle can be won. It has become an obsession to many. But most of these attempts at stilling the enemy within only work for a while, giving us ammunition to use in battle but never enough to win the war. After a time, our unhealthy, one-sided, one-way attempts at relationships backfire. We lose not only the outer battle for love, acceptance, and attention but also the inner battle of self-worth, self-esteem, and value.

Many codependents redouble their efforts and manipulation to gain approval, love, or attention. They start a new campaign by trying to find more love from without. It rarely works for long.

This is what makes codependency so devastating. It creates a no-win situation. It becomes the ongoing battle of life, dominating a struggle for worth, identity, value, and esteem.

Codependence Is a Wounded Heart's Cry for Love

Many addictions are a facade for codependency. Codependents overeat, drink excessively, become sexually obsessed, gamble, grow more depressed, and even kill themselves to win the war and stop the pain. Why does all this cause people to violate the laws of love and relate codependently? The key causes are seemingly, and perhaps surprisingly, the same root issues behind any powerful problem.

Genetics or Bloodline Sets the Stage

One of the important principles we all need to remember is that we are who our parents were. We received our basic nature from our parents. Their genetic codes are imprinted on us, and therefore we are going to be very much like them. Codependency is a set of behaviors or characteristics that for many seem to come embedded in their nature. More and more evidence is accumulating on how our basic predispositions are set at birth.

Ever notice how one baby enters the world crying and never seems to stop while another is peaceful, calm, serene? Children are different even from birth. Though we don't know how it all works, we do know that genetics plays a major role in setting the stage for most emotional or behavioral problems. Even if raised in separate environments, twins from an alcoholic family grow up having a higher probability of becoming alcoholic than kids without alcoholic ancestors. Their genetics seem predisposed to alcoholism if they drink. But this is the way most things work. Anger runs in families; so do depression and even sexual response patterns. Adopted kids are known to still carry the anger, fear, or other predominant traits of their birth parents.

The Scriptures talk of the sin nature being passed down through the bloodline. This means the tendency in all of us to do wrong comes from our nature. Our nature comes from our parents. Our parents' patterns of living, loving, and caring will be, in great part, built into our nature.

This is why a spiritual rebirth is vital to overcoming any life-dominating problem. A new nature is needed. A spiritual awakening provides the new strength, hope, direction, and life that is contrary to the old nature and its given tendencies.

Codependency for many will be a built-in tendency. It

will be in the child's nature to want to please, to want to give or care for others. The events of life and family dynamics will either encourage or discourage the tendency. Many children, though from alcoholic parentage, don't become alcoholics. The events of life and their inner responses have kept them from drinking. If you don't drink, you can't become an alcoholic.

Family Dynamics Mold the Pattern of Response

Our families are the learning labs of life. How we get our needs fulfilled shapes how we respond to those needs as well as the needs of others. Families are powerful forces in shaping our frames of reference for love and need fulfillment.

Fear of rejection, inclusion, affirmation, acceptance, affection, and attention are all important needs, which are first fulfilled in relationships within the family structure. If Mom and Dad aren't managing their own needs well, they will mismanage the needs of their children. This makes for a dysfunctional family.

Codependency comes from wrong need fulfillment. The child is wounded by the lack of love, care, or attention or even by being given love in a wrong or distorted way. This sets the codependency pattern. Alcoholic families are breeding grounds for codependence. So are other dysfunctional family environments. In alcoholic homes, Mom and Dad are too preoccupied with booze to love the kids rightly. If Dad's the alcoholic, the kids usually lose his love, affection, and attention and may even incur his abuse or neglect. Mom is also wounded and unable to relate to the kids rightly. She will make them too important or not important enough or both. Either way, the home is not the stable, safe, and loving place it needs to be.

A parent with too much anger, workaholic tendencies, sexual obsessions, passivity, emotional problems, or even religious addiction can set the stage for imbalance and dysfunction in the family, which in turn creates codependency. Anything that detracts from healthy family life will affect the children.

Dysfunctional families usually create codependency. If the tendency in the child was already present, the dysfunctional family will powerfully set those emotional patterns into action.

The Events of Life Precipitate or Reinforce the Codependency

Significant events in life can make the codependency come alive or bring the existing pattern to a head. Sexual molestations, incest, and physical abuse are all powerful events. They can precipitate codependent patterns. Other events that wounded us, such as a lost first love or parental rejection, also empower the codependent patterns.

For most, wounding events will add fuel to an already existing tendency. Unresolved losses are especially potent in their ability to fan codependent patterns of response. I had a particularly difficult year in college when I "lost" a lot. It strongly fueled my codependency because I did not resolve the losses.

The challenge of all events in life is how we respond to them. Codependents are usually still unhealed on the inside. The outer events have caused inner bruises. The inner bruises have not healed. The inner wounds fuel and drive the codependent pattern.

The Enemy within Is Both Cause and Result

When we look at the result of codependency as well as the cause, the focus comes back to us and our inner self. Somewhere deep within us is a damaged or wounded inner being, flawed by the presence of an enemy. The voice of this enemy can have many expressions, but the message will always be the same—somehow we are the unlovables, the untouchables, the unworthy or not valuable. The voice is a self-doubting, accusatory, and self-depreciating one. It will always be a voice *against* us. There will be no hope or redemption in it. The emotional results of the voice are also predictable. We feel insecure, inferior, inadequate, and even ashamed. All of these are self-rejecting states of inner existence that motivate us to make decisions and act in ways that will compensate for or overcome the negative voice and feelings.

Codependency emanates from here. It comes from deep within us, from our inner spirits. It is a desperate need for love, care, affection, belonging, affirmation, or attention. The need comes from our self-hate and results in self-love. We become too focused on our need for love. We love, care, and give too much for the wrong reasons. We end up in one-way relationships and don't know how to manage them. We set ourselves up for failure because we spend too much time dealing with all the people "out there" whom we love and need love from, instead of focusing on our own "inner being," to get at the roots of our enemy within. To be healed of the wounds of our childhood. To adopt new rules for love and life.

The "Inner Child" Can Help Us Change

Is codependency a hopeless affliction with no answers? Absolutely not! I have changed and witnessed many others change. Change requires three essential steps:

1. Recognition and ownership of the codependency. It's necessary to recognize our codependence and realize we are the ones who need change.
2. Learning what healthy relationships are all about to establish a pattern or goal to work toward.
3. Dealing with the root issues of our past that require healing and change. The enemy within needs to be exorcised; the wounds and losses, healed; the shame and secrets of our life, released; and our old nature, subjected to the power of a new spiritual one.

How we accomplish these three things can vary. Each person must find an individual path to healing. Wherever you are now, trust God to unveil that path.

For many, the concept of our "inner child" will be helpful to focus the change or healing. The inner child of our past is a representation of parts of our childhood that have been unresolved or unhealed. We all have been hurt as children.

For many of us there are still wounds going back to when we were five years old. The five-year-old child whose wound was not healed still resides in us, reacting out of that old, open hurt. It's necessary for us to deal with the aching child within, one who needs God's love and attention. There are different "inner children" of the past. Each represents a part of us we still need to face.

Sobbing, Hurting Child

The hurt-filled or wounded part of each of us may not have healed from wounds of loss or rejection. There are still tears to shed and pain to surrender.

Angry, Defiant, or Rebellious Child

The offended part of us responds to the injustice and unfairness by striking back. It's the part of us that cries out for justice, for love, attention, or acceptance.

Hidden, Lonely, Depressed Child

The offended and hurt part of us strikes inward instead of out. This part finds solace and comfort in self-pity and withdrawal.

Shamed, Embarrassed Child

This part of us fundamentally rejects who we are. It is painfully self-conscious and self-doubting. It kills our desire to live, create, and rejoice in all of creation.

Scared Child

The fearful past causes us to be robbed of life by our worries, fears, concerns, and confusion. We don't want to risk.

As you can see, each of these is merely a way of labeling unresolved and unhealed parts from the past that continue through today. We are codependent because our inner child of the past is still unresolved within us, still hurting, angry, scared, rebellious, or ashamed.

For others, healing will come as we remember the

events or experiences that wounded us or as we mourn the losses never fully faced. For each person, the journey may be different.

There is, however, one more necessary step to healing codependency. It relates to the first and highest law of love and relationships. It is the other law of love which all codependents have violated: "Love the Lord your God with all your heart and with all your soul and with all your mind." This law of love sets the reference point for how all love must begin. Our first reference and greatest love must be God. Codependents love, give, and care for others much more than they care for God. They fill their inner being with thoughts, feelings, and desires for everyone else but God. Sometimes they are even unaware of how much He loves and cares for them.

No one is ever loved perfectly. We all have unfulfilled needs. We are like empty cups needing to be filled. When we attempt to fulfill our deepest need for a love relationship with people, experiences, or things instead of God, it will not work, and we can become codependent or addicted.

Our cups need to be filled first with God's love through a personal spiritual awakening. Then the yearning for significance, approval, and acceptance will be fulfilled.

That codependents have been at cross-purposes to the laws of love is reflected in their attitudes and behaviors toward themselves and others. The distortion of the law of love is a condition of all human nature. It is in our bloodlines, families, and culture. Facing ourselves, our pasts, and God brings healing and hope for the future.

Chapter 6

Deep within each of us is a core belief system that directs our life. These deep inner attitudes and beliefs are made up of our judgments and evaluations of the world, the people around us, and ourselves. We register an inner imprint in response to the circumstances around us, whether positive or negative. We must reexamine these imprints to begin healing and to imprint new patterns of wholeness.

6 The Remarkable Power of Imprinting

I BET HE FELT FOOLISH walking around the back yard with the baby ducks following. He flapped his arms like wings, and they imitated him. What would the neighbors have said had they seen him? But it won him a Nobel prize in 1973.

Konrad Lorenz was a zoologist studying animal behavior. He raised baby ducks as part of his experimentation. Just as the eggs began to hatch, he quickly removed Mama Duck and placed himself next to the ducklings, who bonded to him as though he were Mom. When he waddled across the yard, they followed. They tried to go everywhere he went. However, as the ducklings matured, a noticeable problem set them apart: They did not waddle normally. Having Lorenz as their "mother" had affected them. Because he was unable to imitate a duck's waddle totally, his progeny never learned the correct procedure. They were indeed strange ducks because they had bonded to a man and patterned their behavior on him instead of on their natural mother.

This led to the discovery that ducks and animals have developmental timetables wherein they learn to establish and refine certain behaviors that are common to their species. Ducks have a developmental timetable of only a few hours after birth in which to bond to their mother and learn to be proper ducks. Not having a mother duck available, Lorenz's ducks bonded to him and never developed properly. It was also learned that the developed behavior could not be established before or after the special timetable. If Lorenz replaced the mother hours after birth, the ducklings still developed normally. Replacement had to occur during the critical time of development.

The process of fully establishing behavioral patterns or traits became known as imprinting. The ducks imprinted on Lorenz instead of Mom. The imprint or brand of his influence was firmly established in their lives during that crucial time.

This developmental principle has a lot to do with code-pendency. It is a major factor in explaining why some of us love, care, or give too much for the wrong reasons. We have been imprinted during certain crucial developmental periods of our life. For many codependents specific events have triggered or fully established the wrong pattern or trait of loving, caring, or giving too much. Those events imprinted them, and since then they have been responding according to the imprints.

Traumatic Imprints

One of the most common negative imprintings in life for women was at the root of Sally's codependency. As we met one day for counseling Sally described a bothersome dream she'd had a few nights before. A man was chasing a little girl. The man was naked, and the little girl wore a beautiful new dress that was soiled in front and back. The dream had come for the third time, each time more vividly. I asked her if she had ever been molested or raped. This brought tears to her eyes and a gradual recollection of being molested at the age of five by an uncle. The man in the dream was her uncle, and she was the little girl. The soiling on the dress represented her uncleansed shame.

Sally had mentioned the molestation to her mother when it first happened. Her mom reacted with astonishment, telling her to not say such bad things about other people. Sally felt more ashamed and scared. When she was nine, an older neighborhood boy also touched her in private areas, but she was too scared to resist him and too ashamed to tell anyone.

Shameful events like these are powerful in how they imprint a person's future response in relationships. The power of the imprint seems to be directly related to the following variables:

Emotional Vulnerability

Sally, at age five, was emotionally impressionable. Sexual molestation is a powerful and scary happening to a five-year-old. Her uncle had exposed his private parts to her and demanded that she kiss them and fondle them. A twenty-year-old woman has a better ability to process the shame of such a thing than does a five-year-old or a scared nine-year-old. The stage of life and emotional vulnerability of the person being imprinted makes the effect more or less powerful. Little children have a limited ability to fully understand and resolve issues like this all by themselves. However, they feel the full force of the emotional impact as greatly, if not more so than adults.

Childhood memories are usually our most vivid recollections. As we grow and mature, we sort through the experiences of life better. The more vulnerable the person, the more potential for adopting a wrong imprint of how to love, care, or give as well as how to respond to someone else's loving, caring, or giving.

The Power of the Event

Some events are intrinsically more powerful than others. A traumatic sexual event usually makes a more powerful impression than other events. Sex is powerful stuff. The nature of the sexual abuse also makes a difference. If her uncle had penetrated her, it would have been even more traumatically violating and the imprint more negatively powerful. If he had only slightly touched her, the imprint would not have been as frightening.

The more powerful the event, the deeper the scar of the imprint and the more serious the effects. The molestation at five years of age was much more powerful than the one at nine which reinforced the imprint of fear, shame, and confusion that was already there.

The Person Involved

The closer and more bonded emotionally one is to the person involved in a negative imprint, the more powerful and confusing the result. It was especially difficult for Sally to deal with the molestation because her uncle was her favorite in the family; therefore he was trusted. He was a young teenager at the time and showered her with lots of attention and even little gifts on occasion. To have someone who was so close violate her caused real confusion and self-doubt. The closer the person to you, and the more natural a part of your life, the greater the confusion about what happened.

This confusion hinders healthy sorting out of the experience. Should too many mixed messages get imprinted, the child develops a conflicting and distorted inner evaluation of what sex, family, love, attention, and closeness are all about. Incest is so very difficult because what is sick is portrayed as normal. The person's closeness to the child creates a more powerful potential for mixed-up understanding of how to love, care, or give to others.

The Reaction of Significant Others to the Event

Sally's mom responded in the wrong way. She made the negative imprint worse by making Sally feel she had done something bad or wrong in saying anything about her uncle. This had the effect of making things even more confusing. It made Sally unsure about whether her uncle had really done something wrong. It also made her more ashamed of herself. Shame makes us doubt ourselves, blame ourselves, and not deal rightly with the truth or our own reactions. What others say or do not say to us regarding a traumatic event helps seal what we say to ourselves. The most important aspect of human imprinting is the inner response we make to the outward event. What Sally said to herself deep within is what determined her future responses to sex, her uncle, herself, and by generalization, what she later said about love, boyfriends, men, and relationships. The messages are all connected, and the imprint usually begins with negative traumatic events or highly positive events that set our inner responses in motion.

In the inner response to the outward events we register the imprint. Deep within each of us is a core belief system that directs our life. These deep inner attitudes and beliefs are made up of our judgments and evaluations of the world, the people around us, and ourselves. These inner beliefs are also made up of inner pledges we make to ourselves regarding how we feel about the events of life. These inner pledges are called inner vows. Sally had a hard time truthfully evaluating the molestation. Mom did not help her and actually made her feel worse. It was even more difficult to evaluate or judge rightly because of her age and the uncle's favored status. All these feelings led to deep inner evaluations that were untruthful and hence harmful. These are the inner evaluations we discovered as she and I went back to the event and re-sorted the experience and her inner response:

- "It's all my fault."
- "Something is wrong with me for being so upset."
- "It's no big deal; my uncle was just loving me."
- "If I do not let him do what he wants, he will not like me anymore."
- "I cannot trust myself to know if it is right or wrong."

Based on these and other inner evaluations, she then made deep inner vows to herself, which were especially damaging because they would later set in motion her future responses. All inner vows are powerful because they are promises we make to ourselves to react or respond in certain ways. We want to believe the vows will protect us from being hurt again. Sally's inner vows were:

- "I will never make such a big deal again about someone wanting sex."
- "I will never complain again to Mom."

As Sally grew, these vows added to other vows she was making in response to her dad's anger and her mom's need for comfort. The added vows and evaluations were:

- "It is my fault if I make Dad angry."
- "I will do whatever Dad wants so he won't be angry with me."
- "Mom needs me to make her feel better."
- "I will do anything Mom wants to keep her from hurting."

When these inner vows and judgments add up, they represent an inner attitude toward relationship that was imprinted by the early molestation and ongoing family dynamics. She developed an inability to trust her own perceptions about what was right or wrong in a relationship and to say no to inappropriate demands or requests. Fearful of displeasing others, she wanted to keep others from hurting at any cost.

These attitudes were further imprinted or solidified in her late teen years with Bob, her first lover and first husband. The teen years are especially critical for relationship development. They are, therefore, powerful times of relational imprinting. First loves and lovers establish patterns of loving that continue with us throughout our life.

Bob was a high school football star from an alcoholic home. He played hard and partied a lot. On a chance occasion Sally ended up talking to him after a football game. A few drinks later Bob put the move on her by giving her his standard sob story. She fell for it and a few hours later was having sex with him in the car, even though she really did not want to. She was an accident waiting to happen. Her core beliefs set her up to feel sorry for him. She wanted to fix him just as she always fixed her mom's wounds. She needed to be needed. She also could not say no to his sexual advances because her inner beliefs made her afraid to say no. She doubted her instincts about what was right to do in the situation. With the loss of trust and dignity resulting from long-term, pent-up emotional problems, she felt she had no alternative.

The sexual encounters were repeated until she got pregnant. She desperately wanted to marry him to escape her worsening home situation and take care of her guilt and shame. Bob gave in to the pressure and they were married.

These were Sally's codependent roots. Her tendency to love, care, and give too much for the wrong reasons came from the imprints of her past. They set the pattern in motion for her one-way, unhealthy relationships.

Each of us must reexamine these imprints to bring healing and to imprint new patterns of wholeness. We have to let go of our unhealthy past to establish right patterns for the future. Sally was responding to the present as though it were the past because she was "stuck" in the muddied imprint of the past.

Sally's healing was dramatic. We revisited the scene of her molestation. She relived the fear, doubt, and shame that had never been resolved. We talked about it, and I had her describe it in detail. But not just to me. I had her tell Jesus all about it. As she did, the tears came and the shame left. The facts did not change, but her inner vows did. She saw how she had made wrong evaluations about the situation and how her promises to herself were also wrong.

She was able to see how wrong her uncle had been. The anger came, but then it left and she forgave. She had to recognize that she was angry with him, and that her anger was legitimate, before she could *freely* forgive him. Recognizing and turning from the vows and judgments released a new freedom in her. She felt forgiven by God for her wrong and self-defeating vows, cleansed of her shame, and released from the tormenting memory. She was even able to work through her feelings about her mom and forgive her. This brought significant change to her inner responses, which gives her the ability to make different choices today.

Sally and I spent other times together in prayer, going through her relationship with Bob, Phil, her father, and again her mother. All brought change and healing.

There are other key imprinting events in the life of a codependent that can set the stage or establish the pattern of loving too much for the wrong reasons. Throughout this book I will continue to describe those root imprints, their effects, and how to be healed.

How the Healing Comes

There is a pattern to how the healing comes when we deal with imprints from the past. In His way, God heals these difficult negative patterns. The essential ingredients are:

Revelation

The revelation of the imprinting events or circumstances can come through prayer, discussion, dreams, or even by someone else's felt sense of what God may be telling him or her about you.

Reexamination

There is a reexamination and reexperiencing of the event. These open the door to discovering the wrong evaluations or judgments made and isolating the self-defeating inner vows.

Prayer

Prayer is then used as the power for change. Facing Jesus in prayer releases His love, care, truth, and healing. The ugly wounds are divinely touched, the fear is gone, and the shame is released. He gives the power to change as we are willing to face what needs to be changed.

Forgiveness

Forgiveness is both received and given. The wrong judgments and vows are offered to Him to forgive and empower change. A friend of mine calls these judgments and vows "lies and orders." They are lies we have told ourselves and orders to act we have given to ourselves based upon the lies. Jesus' truth destroys the lies and our surrender to Him gives new and healthy orders. Our forgiveness of others is essential. The forgiveness, however, must be real and deep. It cannot be superficial or only a verbalized statement. The anger and hurt must be fully processed before the forgiveness is given. This kind of healing forgiveness is rare, because it is a giving up of our rights, our defenses, our hurts. It is a promise to ourselves and to others not to bring up the offense again to them, to others about them, or even to our own thoughts. True forgiveness is a true letting go of the past; forgiveness is the only release for bitterness, resentment, and wounds or the sins of others against us. For some the wound will be so deep that you will need God to help you forgive. Jesus was able to forgive those who hurt Him so deeply. Ask Jesus to give you that same power to forgive others that He showed on the cross.

The following words written by a Jew were found in a concentration camp after World War II and published in the French weekly *Dinoche*.

Peace be to men of bad will, and an end to all revenge and to all words of pain and punishment.
So many have borne witness with their blood!
O God, do not put our suffering upon the scales of Thy justice.
Lest it be counted to the hangman, lest he be brought to answer for his atrocities.
But to all hangmen and informers, to all traitors and evil ones, do grant the benefit of the courage and fortitude shown by those others, who were their victims. . . .
Grant the benefit of the burning love and sacrifice in those harrowed, tortured hearts, which remained strong and steadfast in the face of death and unto their weakest hour.
All this, O Lord, may it count in Thine eyes, so that their sin be forgiven.
May this be the ransom that restores justice.
And all that is good, let it be counted, and all that is evil, let it be wiped out. . . .
May peace come once more upon this earth, peace to men of good will;
And may it descend upon the others also.

AMEN

Share your heart totally with God. Ask Him to reveal and heal. Speak your forgiveness of others out loud in prayer. Ask Him to forgive you for any wrong responses on your part. Acknowledge to Him the vows you have made out of hurt, anger, fear, and guilt. Release them to Him, asking for His power to break their hold over your life. Especially ask Him to take away the pain and empower forgiveness. If you are stuck in an area, pray for His revelation. It will come.

The losses you have suffered especially need His grace. We all lose something or someone at some time. The more investment and security we had in the person, place, animal, or thing, the greater the loss. Loss directly tests our ability to "let go and let God be God."

Surrender all your losses to Him. The more you let go of your losses, the more of Him you gain. The more you surrender of your own ways, the more of His you can enjoy.

Embracing Truth

A new inner message of truth is adopted. This can come by embracing and confessing a Scripture verse or a statement that represents God's clear evaluation of the situation as well as God's direction for action. It is a reprogramming of our inner attitudes and core beliefs. The other steps brought the healing and release. This step adds the necessary ingredients for continued health.

It can be dangerous to be rigid about steps like these that can lead to healing. My concern is that God does not always do these steps in the order I have given. Healing can start with any one of the steps and progress through the rest. What I've presented is the most common sequence but not the only one.

One thing is sure; prayer is a first step that is never wrong. If codependency and one-way relationship patterns are a problem in your life, pray! Pray for a revelation of how you were imprinted. Ask Jesus to help you work through the steps as we walk through this book together.

Remember, He is able if you are willing. He is faithful. Do not be afraid.

Chapter 7

To deal with codependency in depth, we must understand our family roots. Family is the single most powerful influence in shaping our relationships.

7 The Imprint of Codependency Began in Your Family

FAMILIES ARE GENERATIONAL. Our families are our link with the past and our bridge to the future. What happens in my family will have a direct effect on my children's families and their families. What happened in my father's and mother's families and their families of origin has affected them and me. This is a fact of life.

Codependency runs in families. It is a family problem that is passed down from generation to generation. The Scripture says that the sins of the fathers are passed on to the children even to the third and fourth generation.

Codependency or any problem needs to be examined in the light of its family origins. Relational problems like codependency do not just appear out of nowhere. They are cultivated in the incubator of family life and are triggered by the wounds of rejection and loss.

A popular country and western song expresses it this way: "Like father, like son; like mother, like daughter. What is sown by the one is grown by the other."

To deal with our codependency in depth, we must understand our family roots. Family is the single most powerful influence in shaping our relationships. If you want to know why you are having problems in relationships, look at your family origins first. It is in our family relationships that we develop a sense of how to relate to others and ourselves. Out of our family life we develop the patterns of giving, caring, and loving that make up our framework of love in relationships. But for many, family is sacred territory, not easily open to examination.

I have interviewed people who have been abused physically, sexually, and emotionally. I have asked them, "What is your family like?"

They say, "I have a really neat family."

"Tell me about your mom."

"She's a good woman."

"What about your dad?"

"Oh, he's okay too."

I explore further. "Tell me, how did your mom treat you?"

"Okay, I guess. She worked hard all the time just to provide for us."

"Did she love you, hold you, care for you?"

"Not really."

"What about your dad?"

"He drank too much."

Slowly but surely, people start describing the hurtful parts in their families. On the surface the family was great: Mom was the greatest; Dad was the greatest, but underneath there are still hurtful wounds and disappointments.

For most people there is a real hesitancy to look at their family closely. Some feel disloyal if they say something bad about their families, a carryover of one of their family rules. There is a truth to this rule. We do not need to broadcast all our family insufficiencies to the world. However, it can also be an unhealthy rule when it keeps you from facing the truth about yourself and your family. It is always unhealthy to hide the truth from yourself.

Another hesitancy in opening up our family lives to scrutiny is the fear of being perceived as heaping the blame for all our problems on family. We are afraid someone will say, "You're just trying to blame your family for your own problems." The value of seeing our family's sickness is neither to blame nor to excuse them. It is to honestly appraise what happened and is happening so that we can see how we became who we are in order to change.

How we love, care, and give has everything to do with our family origins. It also has to do with other events in life that added to or detracted from the imprint. The more we understand family life and specifically our family imprints, the more we will be able to love, care, and give in healthy ways.

Family imprints us in three interesting and powerfully important ways. The first is in our perception of ourselves. Psychologists call this self-concept. Self-concept is the sum total of all the thoughts, beliefs, images, and perceptions we have about ourselves. Therefore, it deals with how we value ourselves, how we see ourselves, how we understand ourselves. How our family related to us helped shape how we relate to ourselves. Critical parents or angry family members project the message that "something is the matter with you." Caring, attentive parents are, by their actions, saying, "You count; you're valuable." How your family treated you had much to do with what you ended up thinking about yourself. If your family was critical rather than nurturing, you will probably have a negative self-concept.

Self-concept is important because your self-worth will guide who you relate to as well as how you relate. If you feel unworthy and have a negative self-concept, you will relate to others out of a fear of being rejected. Thus you will do and say things to be accepted and avoid rejection. You will love, care, and give too much for the wrong reasons.

The second thing family imprints is your perception of other people. Are other people kind? Are other people generous? What are people like? The first exposure you have to evaluating others will be in your family. Your family will interpret for you what other people are like. Moms and dads are always saying, "Look, that person is good, but this person is bad. She is nice, but he's a rat," and so on. They say it openly with words or indirectly by their actions. Your family is going to help define how you perceive other people. How you feel about rich people, poor people, white people, black people, and so on. The root of racism in all of us stems first from our families.

How you view others in relation to yourself determines what you will do with them and to them. If your mother saw men as untrustworthy and you by extension agree, then you will view men the same way. You will never fully trust, surrender, or become intimate with the man of your choice. It can also provoke untrustworthiness in others. What we fear from others will pressure them to respond in wrong ways.

A Framework for Love

The third thing your family imprints is your framework for love. Framework for love is an interesting concept. It says that in every person there is a framework, a reference base, or an idea of what love is understood to be, which means that you have certain behaviors and ideas about what it is like to receive love. You also have certain beliefs about what it is like to give love. That's your framework of love.

Giving Things

For some, giving love means giving things. You ask them, "Do you love me?" Instead of answering yes, they give you something. This is their way of saying I love you.

I have an aunt who is only four feet, ten inches tall. One of the neat things about her short stature was how all of us kids were able to measure our own rate of growth by her. The minute we were taller than Aunt Ercell, we knew we were almost grown up.

Many people like to bless others by giving. For them, when it stems from a pure heart, it is healthy. My aunt has an unusual gift of giving. She shows everybody how she loves them by giving them things. Uncle Bob used to shake his head and say, "I don't even know why she works for a paycheck." On payday she often owed more than she made to the store where she worked. She was always giving treats and even necessities to people. She loved to treat us kids at work and did this for years. Her framework of love was to give.

Affirmations

Other people's framework of love is not giving things. It

is giving touches or pats, or it is giving affirmation by saying, "You are neat," "You're cute," or "I like you." Everyone has a personal style.

Every family has a style too, and your style developed out of your family's. It developed so that either you continue to follow the pattern or, disliking the way your family did it, you do the opposite.

This is one of the imprinting truths about family. Family shapes you one way or another, either by what you do that is the same or by your judgment against it and your desire to be different. Your family will stir you to one of these two responses.

If your family had well-established patterns of caring, loving, or giving too much, then you probably also have those patterns in your framework of love. You learned them from your family. Or you learned them in response to a lack of love, care, or concern in your family. Later events in life reinforced the patterns, but they began as you developed your framework of family love.

Overcoming codependency requires facing the healthy and unhealthy parts of our families or origins. What did your family teach you about relationships? What your family modeled is what you will imitate or react against. Children love to imitate their moms and dads. To children, parents are like gods. The way their parents do things is the way they want to do things. We have all seen little kids imitate: wanting a screwdriver because Dad has one; or wanting to stir the batter for the cake because Mom stirs it. They learn through imitating. They learn through observing and repeating what they see.

But children learn another way too. They learn by judging against what they see when what they see causes pain, difficulty, hurt, or loss. They judge against it and vow to themselves never to be like that. How many times have we all heard a rebellious and hurting teenager say "I don't want to be like you" or "I will never marry a man like Dad" or "I'll never let a man do that to me"?

Each of us has deep within us inner vows that we have

made about the hurting things in our life. We have made inner promises or pledges to ourself never to be like that, do what they did, live the way they lived. Counselors call these inner judgments and vows "self-preserving defenses against pain." Like most defenses they help for the moment, but they cause problems over time. They are usually born out of hurt, anger, and bitterness. They keep us from resolving the hurt that is really there and instead direct us in paths to compensate for the hurt, cover up the hurt, or avoid future hurt. They rarely work and lay the foundation of codependent patterns of loving, caring, or giving.

What Mom and Dad do will set the stage for what we believe about ourselves and how we relate to others. If we are not given attention as a child, we may imitate our parents and not give others attention. Or we may judge against them and constantly strive to get the attention we never enjoyed. Or we may even feel awkward receiving attention but have no problem giving others our full attention. It depends upon whom we imitate and what we judge against.

My friend who is always nice had vowed to herself to be nice so that no one could be angry or critical with her. Her niceness was a defense mechanism to ward off her dad's anger and disapproval. On a deeper level she became nice because she vowed to never be like her father. She despised him and the way he hurt and wounded others. There was no acceptance in her family, only anger and rejection. She vowed to be different.

I met her mother last year and found her to be charming and very nice. The two of them were more like sisters than mother and daughter. It struck me that not only had she vowed not to be like Dad but she had also imitated Mom. Mom was also a pleasure, very nice, and Mom tiptoed around Dad to keep the peace. Mom affirmed through placating and people-pleasing. Mom avoided confrontation and conflict so there would be no anger and uproar. Mom never handled the truth truthfully. Mom's codependence got passed on to my friend, her daughter, through imitation and judgment. My nice friend even married a man who acted much like her father. I have wondered about her young daughter. Will she imitate Mom and judge against Dad, or will she imitate Dad and judge against Mom? This is how it works in all of us. Each of us, as we are raised, both imitates and judges. We try to be like one or the other parent or vow not to be like those who wound and hurt us or the ones we care for. The combination of imitation and judgments sets the pattern in all life for relationships in the future. Our choices about whom we marry, whom we have as friends, and what we do with those close to us will be based on our limitations and judgments, based on old family patterns and needs.

My family pattern of codependency is similar to one that is now widespread in single-parent homes. My mother gave me a lot of attention and affection as I grew up. I returned that attention by meeting my mother's emotional needs through my accomplishments and my willingness to share my heart with her. Because of the conflict between Mom and Dad, I felt sorry for Mom and tried to make her feel better. I tried to perform and succeed so that she would be happy. I knew that she was disappointed in her marriage and disappointed with her lot in life. It became my goal to overcome her disappointment. I became a surrogate partner for my mom. I wanted her to live out her dreams through me. This provoked me to judge against my dad for not meeting my mom's emotional needs. The result was a pattern of codependent relating laid from the early stages of my life.

I developed a need to be needed. I got strokes for being the good boy, the achiever, the one who cared. Because I was needed by my mom, I wanted to be needed by others. I wanted especially to be needed by women. I felt badly whenever my mother was upset, and I wanted to fix it for her. I also ended up feeling badly whenever my wife was upset, wanting to fix her. My vows destined me to choose a wife who was needy, whom I could help fix emotionally. I tried to be the strong one. I promised things I could not fulfill. I disappointed my wife. Realizing she was disappointed, I redoubled my efforts and blamed her for not responding.

The codependency that I saw in my relationship with

my dad was also being lived out in my relationship with my wife. I needed to go back and resolve my issues of rejection with my dad and my inner vow to keep my mother—and by extension, all women—from being disappointed. Lastly, I needed to release the judgment against myself that something was the matter with me if I failed to keep someone else from being disappointed. The root of the issue was my own need to be needed, my own need to gain worth by pleasing and fixing others.

Single-parent, divorced, or separated families are especially prone to this pattern. The custodial mother's disappointment and disillusionment with her husband can translate into getting her emotional needs met through her sons or daughters. This provokes the child to want to fix Mama's disappointment, to want to keep her from hurting any more, to make sure Mama is okay. This pattern creates codependency, the pattern of needing to be needed, the pattern of needing to fix others in order to gain worth or value in your own life, the pattern of bearing someone else's burdens you were never equipped to bear. Children are not able to bear the emotional burdens and traumas of their parents. The effort to do so confuses them and stirs unhealthy and hurtful inner responses. Children are not to be substitutes for what the marriage relationship lacks. The needs of each marriage partner must be met by the other, not by the children.

In the United States in the past thirty years we have severely wounded an entire generation of children through separation and divorce. In the 1950s, 70 percent of all homes were occupied by traditional families—original Mom, original Dad, and their children. Seven out of ten homes on an average block in America were made up of traditional families.

Now, only 15 percent of the homes on an average block in America are composed of the original Mom, original Dad, and kids. The rest are occupied by single individuals, single-parent families, childless couples, and blended or recombined families. These families have a mom from one family and a dad from another family, with kids from either parent or both. I have even seen families where kids were from

Mom, kids were from Dad, they had kids of their own, and then they divorced. One or the other got custody of all the children and remarried. This new family now has children who do not belong biologically to either parent.

Blended or recombined families, like single-parent families, are natural spawning grounds for codependency. When different parents and children are linked together by marriage, the bonding patterns of the family require a serious effort to remain healthy. The needs of each member of the family will require special attention. Parents have allegiances to their own children, not the new kids. The new father may be confronted with a sexually mature, attractive stepdaughter who wants and needs attention; the mother, with wounded teenage sons she did not bear or raise. Different imprints of values, conduct, and rules are present in each member. Wounds of the past family losses and rejection still need healing. Each of these difficult problems must be faced and resolved by the recombined family. Each family member has deep needs that require fulfillment. Mom and Dad have relational needs for affirmation, acceptance, and affiliation. The kids also have needs of belonging and acceptance.

The way a recombined, single-parent, or any family chooses to meet the needs of each member imprints the pattern of relationships.

Needs are the basic building blocks of relationship and self-fulfillment. A need is a motivating desire for something lacking or something wanted. It is a vacuum in need of filling. We are all born with the above-mentioned needs. How our family meets these needs shapes how we go about relationships in the future.

The challenge for all of us is to learn how healthy families meet these needs. In avoiding codependency it is critical to foster healthy ways of relating. To meet a need in a healthy way means to give enough of what is required to help fulfill the need but, at the same time, not so much that all power is given to meet it. The need is met in a manner that brings fulfillment, not dependency. The need is also met in a way that is morally acceptable and not self-defeating.

This means that each family member must be individually assessed as to need. And each family must have a commonly-ascribed-to philosophy of need fulfillment based on moral rights and wrongs as well as practical know-how.

Lastly, parents need to help the child make the transition from a state of dependent need fulfillment to independent fulfillment wherein the child assumes the responsibility of having needs met through relationship with God.

Right need fulfillment is difficult in healthy families and almost impossible in unhealthy ones. Unhealthy families do not meet the emotional needs of their members, thus fostering unhealthy ways of meeting needs through other people, places, or things. Many of us had a need for family approval that was never met. We ended up seeking peer approval to make up for the lack at home. We bowed to peer pressures that were wrong and unhealthy for us. Wives who do not get their attention or affirmation needs met by their husbands try to get them from their kids. This causes unhealthy patterns.

Other families overdid with each other. They gave too much attention to the need. One of the things everyone requires is attention. Some families give little children too much, causing them to think the whole world is, and should be, focused on them. When they grow up, they expect the world to give them all the attention they got as children. They feel cheated when they do not get it and then try to get it any way they can. Needs constitute one of those really difficult areas you can meet in a healthy way, not meet at all, or meet too much.

Or you can do a fourth thing. You can meet the need in a distorted way. Some siblings get attention only when they are bad. The need for attention becomes distorted in the child. Since negative behavior is the only way they get attention, they grow up needing to be identified as bad or different or radical in order to get their attention needs met.

You will probably find your family as we examine each of these six needs. They met the need in you in a balanced way, did not meet it at all, or met it in a distorted way. The ability to see how your needs were first responded to in your family will give you insight into the need fulfillment patterns you now practice in relationships. It will help you understand, as it helped me, why you love, care, or give too much for the wrong reasons.

Affiliation

First, affiliation. The need for affiliation is the need for belonging and acceptance in a group. Everyone is born with the need to belong, to be attached to somebody or something. Another way of saying it is that everyone has a need to be bonded. To be bonded or attached to someone is a primary relational need. In functional families that are healthy, you will find lasting, positive bonds of mutuality. Notice the characteristics. It is a positive affiliation that benefits both parties. We are bonded or stuck together, attached together in a positive and lasting way.

People need to be stuck together in a long-lasting, stable, or permanent way. They need a secure bond that transcends the ups and downs of life.

When my family blew apart, I did not know where I belonged. When Thanksgiving came, I would think, "Gee, where do I go? Where do I belong?" The first Christmas after the separation was one of the saddest Christmases of my life. My uncertainty over where I belonged kept me from being with any part of my family. The stability of my family bonding was threatened and in flux. I felt insecure and lonely.

Healthy families maintain mutual bonds. Mutual means that both people want the bonding, and they both say they do. How many families do you know in which only one person or one side of the family makes the effort to be attached to the other? It is not mutual. It is not reciprocal. It is one-sided. Our family has this problem. Many of the family patterns of relationship in my family are one-way. They are one-way toward my dad. We initiate contact; we take the responsibility to call, stop by, or give presents. His attachment to us is not mutual.

In a healthy family, attachment is mutual. You go so far, but they also go so far. You move toward them, and they move toward you. It is not you doing all the work. It is not you going all the way. It is not you making all the phone calls and initiating contact. Both do. When the need for affiliation is not rightly met, codependence results. Families that do not bond positively and mutually set in motion codependent patterns of relationship.

Sometimes the only way we can be healthy with our families is to distance ourselves. Sometimes it's the only way because it is all we can handle. Maintain whatever level of attachment and relationship that allows you to be healthy.

Acceptance

Another primary need is acceptance. The need to be accepted—the opposite of being rejected—is powerful in each of us. I do not know of anyone who doesn't want acceptance. And the major, most foundational place you will need acceptance is in your family. You are going to need it from Mom. You are going to need it from Dad. You are going to need it from your brothers and sisters. You are going to want it from your uncles, aunts, grandma, and grandpa. You are going to want it from everyone who is important to you while you're growing up. You are going to want the acceptance given in such a way that it makes you feel on the inside that you're okay. That's what acceptance does. It validates you as worthwhile, makes you feel loved, secure, and valuable. Rejection makes you feel as if you do not count, you are not okay, something is the matter with you. All of us deeply need acceptance.

In families that are healthy you will find acceptance given to every single member of the family, no matter what. In a healthy family, everybody gets accepted. Tall or short, pretty or ugly, good or bad, they get accepted.

You are accepted just on who you are, not on how you look or perform. If you are accepted only based on how you perform and how you look, you are going to try to look better and be better for acceptance. This is a common root of codependence. Not accepting the person provokes loving, caring, or giving in order to win the acceptance—to make up for the lack of acceptance.

In some families you have to be male to be accepted. In other families you have to be a woman, and a pretty one at that, to be accepted. The standard in some families is to be athletic, or maybe in your family you had to be nice and do everything just right to gain acceptance. Cultural and geographical issues have an impact on acceptance. However, conditional acceptance is unhealthy.

Families have a tremendous power of acceptance or rejection. Healthy families accept everyone, regardless. There are no outcasts or black sheep, no scapegoats. Even if you are in prison, you are still accepted. That does not mean that everything you do is acceptable, but you, yourself, are.

A good indicator of a healthy, accepting family is the ability to accept outside the family. Healthy families connect with people from foreign countries; they connect with needy people; they connect with the people next door. Healthy families are not isolated. They do not hide. They do not withdraw. Healthy families know their families, know each other, accept each other, and have enough acceptance to overflow to people of different backgrounds, different races, different colors, different beliefs. Healthy families have a tremendous amount of acceptance. Codependent families lack internal and external exposure.

Attention

Another primary need is the need for attention. In healthy families, everyone gets attention. Not just the girls. Not just the boys. Not just the one who is good at school. Not just the one who is good at athletics. Not just the one who plays soccer. Everybody gets attention—the quiet one as well as the loud one. The kid who is strong-willed gets no more attention than the one who is compliant. Every kid and everybody in the family gets attention. Dad does not get all the attention; neither does Mom. The kids do not get all the attention—everybody gets a full share. That is healthy in a family. *Everybody* gets attention.

Unhealthy families give attention to the child or person they want to reward. The attention is conditional. It can also be negative attention or attention given for wrong or unhealthy reasons. I got too much attention for doing well in school. Too much of it was given out of my family's need for me to be successful. The mixture of motives fed my need for attention in the wrong way. I performed to get attention. I ended up feeling that I would not get attention unless I performed. The need for attention in me was unwittingly fed the wrong way. This helped establish a foundation of codependence. I was performing for the wrong reasons.

Affection

The fourth primary need is for affection. Touching and other demonstrations of affection are natural and continuous in a healthy family. Two key words: natural and continuous. Natural means not exaggerated or forced. They are also not offensive to the other party. The affection is recognized and accepted by all as a sign of affirmation, not a condition based on performance by one person.

The affection is also a way of being in contact with each other. When you are close to people, you touch them. When you are emotionally distant, you do not touch them at all. Every now and then Susan, my wife, and I have misunderstandings that cause emotional distance and offense. In the process of resolving and becoming connected again, there is, first of all, the eye barrier that needs crossing. We need to be able to look again into each other's eyes with kindness and care. But we become fully connected when we cross the touch barrier. When we can start touching again, we know we are reconnected.

There have been times in our family when touching was not easy. It was a tough barrier to cross. A lot of hurt and emotions needed resolution before affection could flow again. Healthy families have touch as a continuous natural part of relationship. Unhealthy families do not touch, or they touch in hurtful or offensive ways.

Affirmation

Another crucial need is for affirmation. In a functional family, everyone is valued. Everybody counts, everyone is affirmed. Healthy families make sure everybody counts. Affirmation is connected to acceptance.

One of the things I appreciate about my wife's family is her ninety-five-year-old grandmother who says she doesn't feel a day over seventy-four. She has been known to do more things in one day than most do in two. She is an accomplished artist, bridge master, and teacher. She took up bowling in her sixties and has trophies. She also has grandchildren, great-grandchildren, and great-great-grandchildren. All four of my kids love Grandma even though we see her only a few times a year. But what endears her most to me is that she knows every one of my children and goes out of her way to make them feel they count.

With Grandma, everybody counts, whether we see her once a year or every day. She affirms the youngest as well as the oldest, the brattiest and the famous ones. The cousins, the aunts, the nephews, and the guests are all welcome at Grandma's home. She has enough love to spread around, and everyone is healthier for it.

I can't help but feel that her kind of affirmation is healthy anywhere. It is healthy whether you are in church, at work, or at home. Unhealthy families make you feel you count only if you measure up to their standard or expectations. This again makes their caring conditional and your loving, caring, or giving codependent.

Unhealthy families convey the message that you never measure up. They undermine your confidence. They become disappointed in you for their sake, not yours. They reject when you disappoint them. This causes self-doubt, shame, and codependence. You will love, care, give, or do to try to gain their confidence so that you can be confident in your-self.

Competence

The last crucial area of need fulfillment relates to our felt need to be able or competent. In a healthy family, every-one is competent. I have wondered if there really is a totally incompetent person. Is there really any such thing as a per-son who doesn't have any abilities, skills, or gifts? I doubt it, unless the person is severely disabled. Yet there are countless thousands who feel incompetent, who have no felt ability. I believe it is most often because no one believed in them. In healthy families, everybody believes in everybody else. Not fantasy beliefs, but real beliefs. Belief that there is some abil-ity, some skill and competency in the person. And it is true. Everybody can do something. Healthy families recognize competency, believe in it, and encourage the person in realiz-ing that gift.

Healthy families do not compare one against the other. The moment you compare, you have lost your belief in that person's uniqueness. Healthy families don't say when look-ing at a son's report card, "Why can't you get As and Bs like your sister?"

When these six needs are rightly fulfilled in families, co-dependent patterns of loving, caring, giving, or doing are greatly minimized or even eliminated. You will survive your family upbringing with a healthy perception of who you are. The self-hate and self-love are held to a minimum. Our view of others and how we relate to them will be balanced. We are taught how to meet needs rightly and how to recognize an-other person's ability to meet our needs.

Last but not least, our framework of love is not self-defeating. We know how to love and be loved for unselfish reasons.

So codependency and addiction are based, in great part, upon what happened in those six areas of need in your life. How healthy was your family? is the question. Healthy families create an atmosphere of belonging and attachment. There is a lot of acceptance, no matter who you are or how you behave. They give attention, affection, and value to each person. Healthy families see each member as competent and able to accomplish something. Healthy families encourage participation, love, honesty, and belonging.

Unhealthy families have difficulty in all these areas. Unhealthy families do not deal with truth truthfully. There is deception and denial. Unhealthy families do not allow kids to feel and explore and deal with their feelings. Unhealthy families also do not trust. Unhealthy families have a lot of unresolved conflict and codependent patterns of relating.

I believe the pattern of codependency will change in the future as more and more men are identified as codependents. This will come in part from their judgment against women, and it will also come about as a result of a major shift that has occurred in our society. More than one million children experience the trauma of separation and loss through divorce each year. There are now more than 13.7 million children under the age of eighteen who live with a single parent. Almost one-fourth of our children live in a home with only a father or mother. These children will make judgments and vows of their own regarding relationships. When the natural needs we all have for affiliation, acceptance, attention, affection, affirmation, and competence are not fully met by both a mother and a father, the children suffer. The deficit of parental love or the distortion of parental love causes difficulty in the children's lives. They will make judgments about their mothers or fathers. They will also judge themselves.

A single parent needs to take positive steps against these negative judgments by not sharing critical judgments of the ex-spouse with the children. Additionally, the children need to understand that they are not at fault for the divorce and don't have to take sides.

Grandparents can help overcome the deficit of love, care, and attention. My dad worked long hours, but my grandpa was always there. He loved me, affirmed me, and spent time with me. His care helped make up for my dad's lack.

Big Brothers, Big Sisters, neighborhood families, friends, and relatives can help. Many of my sons' friends come from single-parent or divorced homes. We make a special effort to include them in family outings. I tell them I love them and let them know they're special. In the same way, your unselfish love can stop a negative pattern from developing any further in a child's life. It can also help heal the wounds.

Codependency and one-way relationships run in families. Codependency is a family problem that is passed down from generation to generation through wounded people whose needs for belonging, acceptance, attention, and affirmation have not been rightly met. We codependents have both imitated and judged our parents and families. The wounds of loss and rejection from our family pasts have become the roots of our codependency. Our judgments and inner vows have fueled the fire of our wounds instead of healing them. Remember, codependency is a wounded heart's cry for love.

Healing codependency is tied to healing the imprint that began in our families. No family is perfect. All of us are susceptible to loving, caring, or giving too much for the wrong reasons. Broken, wounded, or dysfunctional families are especially vulnerable to creating or continuing the sickness of codependency from generation to generation.

Our hope does not reside within us. The deep inner person that is damaged or distorted by unhealthy love requires spiritual healing. We will never be able to satisfy all our needs for love, acceptance, attention, or affection. The vacuum each need represents has to be filled first by God in order to be rightly handled by us.

God at the center of our being guides us in fulfilling the needs. His revealed word is a guideline for life and living. His spirit is a comfort and healing balm to our inner pain. His love is a fulfillment for our deficient family love.

To heal your family imprint, follow the steps given in the

previous chapter on imprinting. If you honestly admit to your family's wrong influence in your life, you have already taken the first step of healing.

Follow the prayer guidelines in the following chapters on wounds, losses, and shame. Each will help bring healing to what you are now recognizing. Have someone else pray with you and for you. Share with a trusted friend. Your deep examination needs time, discussion, prayer, and support from others. God is able if you are willing.

Chapter 8

It hurts to look
at our losses, but
it hurts more not to.

8 What You Lose Can Change Your Life

I SAT IN MY ROOM staring out the window, fighting back tears. It was Christmas 1965, and I was a senior in college. I could not believe it. He had died of a heart attack. My thoughts went back to another special person in my life who had died. He was my grandfather, and he, like Seymour, had loved me with no expectation of return. Seymour had been a high school history teacher who took special interest in me. He believed in me. Now he was dead of a heart attack before the age of forty. My grandpa had also died of a heart attack only a few years before.

I felt all alone. I did not know where to turn or where to go. Because of my mom and dad's sudden separation after years of marriage, I was isolated. Mom moved with four of my younger brothers and sisters to California. Two other younger brothers stayed with Dad, and my oldest brother was in the service. I stayed at school thinking, *Where do I go for Christmas when I don't know where home is any longer?* I was grateful for the invitation from a friend to help out at his dad's guest ranch over the holidays. It gave me an excuse for not having to choose where to spend Christmas.

But something else happened just before this time to make the emotional imprint of the loss unusually powerful. Growing up in a small mining town did not prepare me for the freedom and pressures of a large university. My grades took a nosedive, and I lost my academic scholarship. This was a great disappointment to my mom and dad. My dad, with a fourth-grade education, had worked himself up to the position of smelter foreman of a mining company. His lack of education kept him from the smelter superintendent's job. He prided himself on having a son who attended college on a scholarship. My mom also saw in me the fulfillment of her dreams for a college education. This made my failure their loss. My dad was deeply disappointed in me. To make matters worse, I offended him further by siding with Mom when they separated. This put a new barrier between us.

I had lost my family, my friend, my self-confidence, and now my dad's favor. It was too much to handle. I did what most people do. I denied to myself how important the loss was, how much it hurt, and how greatly I wanted what had been lost. I pushed back the tears and went on with life. But things were different, and my relationship with Dad was not working. This was the beginning of our one-way relationship.

Most codependents who love, care, or give too much for the wrong reasons have unhealed emotional imprints due to loss. I am not unique. Everyone experiences loss. Codependent patterns of relationships can result because few people truly resolve the imprint of grief, disappointment, and fear the losses provoke. The imprinting of those losses during that time of my life affected my relationship choices and patterns for years to come. I did not resolve my grief over the loss.

Grief

Grief is the natural, unavoidable emotional reaction to loss. It is the process wherein we emotionally work through the loss, arriving at a place of true acceptance, a place that says, "I lost and it is okay."

Many codependents have lost but never done their grief work. I did not allow myself to grieve openly or work through the loss. I tried to forget all about it. This made matters worse. My decision to not face the losses was accompanied by deep inner judgments about myself and others, as well as vows to myself that were destined to be self-defeating.

I felt I had to earn the love, attention, and approval I

received. I gave to get; loved to be loved; pleased in order to be accepted. I went the extra mile in relationships so that I would be liked and admired. My deep sense of failure and waning self-confidence needed someone else's approval and support to make me okay. I was disappointed in myself and afraid of losing favor and love again. I needed someone to believe in me because I could not believe in myself. I judged myself a failure, yet I vowed to be invulnerable and strong so that I would not have to face the truth. This caused me to look for weak, lonely, or needy people among whom I could find worth by being the strong one. It also caused me to want too much to regain my dad's lost favor. My self-judgment and vow of invulnerability kept me from having to do my grief work. Judgments and vows are often an excuse for not facing the pain. As Carl Jung has said, "Neurosis is the postponement of legitimate suffering." It hurts to look inside, but it hurts more not to.

Acceptance

The first step in looking at our losses is to get through our denial. Denial is the inner resistance in each of us that does not want to believe the loss has really occurred or that it will mean much to us. Denial says, "Not me—this can't really be happening to me." I minimized the impact by choking back the tears and trying not to think about the losses. The only loss I admitted to was the loss of my scholarship and my failure. But even here, I did not fully resolve. One of my greatest denials was about Mom and Dad's separation. I just could not believe it had really happened. I kept seeing the situation as a temporary dispute that would soon be resolved. It took me more than ten years to accept the permanence of their separation. This is denial.

Anger

Anger is another part of our grief work. When we see what we have just lost, we say, "Why me?" We are offended by having it happen to us. We want to blame. It is not pleasant to lose something you value. It creates anger and hurt. I was angry at Dad and needed to resolve that hurt. I needed to let go of the anger and get on with acceptance. But I denied to myself and others that I was even angry. I also denied I was angry with myself.

The root of my anger was found in disappointment. I was disappointed in myself. I had not lived up to my standard, and I had crushed my parents' hopes. One of the most difficult things for a child to contend with is personal and/or parental disappointment. Disappointment with ourselves lowers our estimate of our own value. Disappointing a parent usually translates into feeling disappointed with ourselves. Unresolved disappointment can have profound effects. It caused me to make codependent relationship decisions. I felt the need to fix Dad's disappointment in me so that I would not be disappointed in myself. The anger and disappointment were empowering my relationship decisions, and I didn't even know it.

Codependents have a lot of unresolved disappointment. We are especially disappointed in ourselves and have never resolved it. The losses of our lives have created much of the disappointment.

Bargaining

We also need to face our tendency to bargain. We say, "Okay, I have lost something, *but . . .*" We want to figure a way out of the loss or a way of trading the loss for something else. We accept the fact of the loss, but only partly. Most bargaining goes on deep within between God and us. We say to Him, "If only you will let me not lose, I'll be good (or different)." We then get angry when He does not respond.

Bargaining never works because it is manipulation directed toward avoiding the consequences of loss. A jilted lover who begs the other person not to leave is not facing the loss but is bargaining—being manipulative to avoid facing the consequences of the loss. It won't work. I never bargained with God over the loss. I was disappointed in Him and too much in denial. I did, however, bargain with myself. I made promises to myself to do better in school, not to disappoint others, and so on. However, I did not keep the bargain.

Boy, did I feel guilty. This was another stage I could not resolve. Guilt is a powerful emotion. It is one of the first emotions we feel when confronted with the loss of someone we love. We wonder if we could have done more or been different. We blame ourselves. I blamed myself. I made deep judgments against myself and vowed to be different. They were the wrong judgments and vows. They were lies and self-defeating orders.

Blame

A major characteristic of all codependents who love, care, or give too much for the wrong reasons is the tendency toward self-blame rather than other-blame. We judge ourselves more at fault than the other person. We find ourselves sorely deficient and cannot work through it to resolution. We get stuck at dealing with our own guilt, so we rarely can deal rightly with the other person. When we lose, we say, "I lost and it's all my fault." I felt guilty for failing. I also unknowingly took on guilt for my parents' separation that was not mine. Researchers have shown this to be a common tendency of children from broken marriages. They feel guilty for the breakup and unwittingly blame themselves.

But there is a subtle, deeper part of this guilt issue that few of us who have codependent traits want to admit. Even though we blame ourselves, we still try to win by being the martyr or victim.

The martyr says, "It is all my fault. I am being wrongly treated, but that's okay; I can take it." It is a sick way of salvaging a measure of self-worth while still feeling guilty. Codependents are martyrs who have never resolved their self-judgment, guilt, and shame issues. I needed to deal with my guilt and martyrdom issues and have them healed. Victims, on the other hand, feel sorry for themselves even though they also, in great part, believe themselves to blame. Victims are full of self-pity and depression to avoid having to take responsibility for any of the loss. In self-pity and depression we say to ourselves, "I have lost and it's hopeless . . . poor me." We cannot get unstuck from the pity we have for ourselves and our wound. There is a payoff to self-pity. Being trapped in the pity pot of depression keeps us from having to take responsibility for getting on with life. It gives us a good excuse to comfort ourselves.

Loss will provoke emotional weakness. If you are prone to self-pity, you will struggle with it when you lose. The imprint of loss will drive the self-pity response deeper unless it is resolved in a healthy way. Those who are anger-prone more often have to deal with resentment. Those who are fear-prone deal with fear.

Fear and guilt are kissing cousins. Guilt is the fear of punishment. When you are fear-prone, you are also guilt-prone and vice versa. When we lose someone important or something precious, we have to face our fear of losing again before resolution is complete. I feared losing more status and favor. I feared abandonment because almost everyone close to me was gone. My guilt-prone nature made the fear worse because I blamed myself. I was afraid of being at fault in a relationship again.

Codependents fear what may happen if they do not do what they think is needed. We put too much responsibility and importance on our actions or inaction. We become too self-centered and obsessed with others. We have not resolved the guilt and fear of our own losses in life. This makes us deal wrongly with others. The imprint of our unresolved loss dooms us to self-defeating, unhealthy relationship choices. A multi-married, well-known entrepreneur said that with every destroyed relationship something within him falls and is never picked up or recovered again. This shows the inner sadness of a man whose wealth has not resolved his loss.

The problem with our losses of people, places, or things is the value each represents to us. Each loss of a person means a loss of love, attention, loyalty, security, or affection. The loss of a place can mean a loss of comfort, familiarity, and support. When we lose someone we love, we lose love. We lose the security that love represented. If you love, care, or give too much for the wrong reasons or find yourself in a one-way relationship, there is a high probability you have not resolved some loss in your life. No one escapes the pain of loss and its imprint if it is not deeply and rightly resolved. One of the first losses most of us experience when young is losing a pet, favored blanket, or special toy. I've heard many stories of deep hurt from those who lost a beloved pet through accident, injury, or circumstance. I also know of individuals who, like Linus in the comics, took great comfort in their blankets. They made them feel secure. It also caused grief when a parent burned the blanket and said it was lost. The grief goes unresolved.

Another loss is moving. In our mobile society, families frequently move to different neighborhoods, cities, and states. A relocation for a child is a significant loss. Familiar surroundings, friends, and habit patterns all change. The high incidence of depression for women in the Sunbelt states has been, in part, a result of moving—leaving behind families, friends, and routines. They start all over again in a place where the sun always shines and there are no seasons. Moving is a significant loss and hard to resolve for many.

The loss of a friend of the family is usually the next loss children have to face. By the time we're teenagers we are usually confronted with the death of a school friend or peer. My ten-year-old son, Andy, had a classmate who died in a freak accident with a go-cart. We were all surprised at the death. It came so unexpectedly. We don't think of third-grade friends dying. Andy needed to talk and pray about the loss. He went through grief, but I am not sure it has all been resolved.

Unexpected losses are the hardest to overcome. As I often share, my parents' separation shocked me. I never thought they would do it. When a friend or loved one dies unexpectedly or out of the normal sequence of loss, it is harder to accept. When we are in our forties and fifties, we begin to think about what it would be like to lose our parents. Even though it is partially expected, the pain of their death will hurt. But if a parent dies when we are younger, it is very hard. My friend Seymour's death was a shock because he was in his thirties. I did not expect the loss.

Another major loss that imprints us relationally comes about in our teens or early twenties. It is the loss of our first love. Do you remember your first love? I do. And so does everyone I have ever asked. First love emotions are powerful. They deeply imprint and affect our view of love, sex, and relationship.

Marilyn had a heartbreaking first-love relationship with a college sophomore named Joe. She was eighteen and not so sure about herself or guys. But Joe seemed so right. He got past her barriers and swept her off her feet. He was everything her dad and other men had never been—friendly, attentive, and caring. He brought her flowers and really talked to her. He appeared in control of himself and his future. He was so exciting. She was overwhelmed with the thought of someone who had it all together caring for her.

The pressure for sex was there from the beginning. She could not resist. She gave herself totally and passionately. And he was gentle and caring. He showered her with affection and promises of love. He called nightly to tell her he loved her before she went to bed.

But things changed. Soon the calls were every three or four nights. But she waited faithfully at home for his infrequent calls. The dates became sexual interludes instead of romantic or fun-filled experiences. She asked him if he still loved her. He said of course, but the bloom of love had wilted. After a week of not hearing from him, she arrived unannounced at his apartment. He was with another date, an older, prettier girl. It crushed her. He was perfect. She felt it was all her fault for not being pretty enough or good enough. She could not see the situation for what it was. His memory haunted her dating relationships for years.

Unwittingly she vowed to never again trust a man or give herself again sexually with such abandon. All her mother's negative judgments against her dad and men now became fully imprinted in her. She could not fully trust. Now she is having problems trusting her husband, Tim. She does not enjoy sex but keeps giving it so that he won't look else-where. She is obsessed with losing the weight she gained dur-ing her pregnancies so that Tim will still think she is pretty. She also is routinely upset with Tim when he is not home on time. She quizzes him on where he has been and with whom. She also makes him report on what women he talked to at work and whom he had lunch with.

Tim lies a lot to avoid trouble. But she has caught him lying, and this has fueled her mistrust and insecurity even more.

Marilyn is reacting to the present as though it were the past. She is caring too much for all the wrong reasons. The loss of the past has created a deep imprint of fear, mistrust, and resentment. She needs to resolve the hurtful loss of the past in order to be free of her codependent pattern of worry, fear, and sexual pleasing.

If not resolved, lost first loves, no matter what the rea-son, leave deep emotional imprints. Many of these imprints then cause us to love, care, or give too much for the wrong reasons.

A lot of research has been done on loss in recent years. Even though loss is something we all must face, some losses are more powerful than others. Researchers have been able to rank the power of one loss over another. Lost loves are especially powerful. The death of a child or that of a spouse is the most difficult loss for an adult. The loss of a parent, family member, friend, or pet is the most difficult for a child to resolve.

Men have difficulty overcoming the loss of a job. Being fired is especially traumatic. Women have difficulty with the loss of their children to adulthood—the empty-nest syn-drome. The children grow up and leave, and Mom has to ad-just to having only Dad around. For many couples, this is threatening. The children have been a buffer for the unre-solved marriage problems. Existing problems that were never addressed finally surface.

Abortion is another powerful loss issue. An unwanted pregnancy can make a woman feel trapped. The pregnancy can mean a loss of freedom, health, or acceptance. Instead of facing those losses, women often choose abortion. What they have done, however, is to trade one unresolved loss issue for another, more powerful one. They now have a deep loss issue coupled with their own responsibility for the loss. It makes the guilt and blame stage of the loss very difficult to resolve. Women cannot deliberately rid themselves of a child and not suffer loss and guilt. These issues can precipitate one-way, codependent relationship patterns.

A beautiful honeydew blonde with unblemished skin, green eyes, and a very feminine physique sat very timidly on the edge of the office couch.

"I can't stop seeing Lonnie. No matter what I tell myself about him, every time he calls, I'm there for him. It's like I'm addicted. What can I do?" she asked.

"Why don't you want to see him?"

"He says he does not want a committed relationship. He just wants to enjoy our sexual relationship and friendship. We have sex whenever he calls, but my conscience keeps telling me it's wrong. He says he won't see me unless we have sex. He says I'm too hung up about it, and if I don't want sex, I shouldn't go out with him. I know I should stop seeing him, but I can't."

She was trapped between her conscience and her strong need for him. We continued the session, and as I listened, I prayed. A deep inner sense prompted me to ask, "Have you ever had an abortion?"

Tears immediately came to her eyes. She sniffed and sobbed. "Yes. I am so ashamed. It was Lonnie's baby, and I didn't tell him. I wanted him to marry me for me, not because I was pregnant. I was also afraid of what my parents would say if they found out. They believe you ought to marry before you have sex."

Gayle was holding on to Lonnie, in great part, out of her guilt. She had not resolved the loss of her abortion.

She had unresolved issues over marriage, premarital sex, and her parents, as well as her own disappointment. She compounded the guilt by choosing an abortion. Her inability to let go of Lonnie came directly from the erroneous assumption that if she could just marry Lonnie, all the guilt issues would be resolved. Her relationship with Lonnie was unhealthy and codependent. She was loving, caring, and giving too much for the wrong reasons. She needed to look at why she was being motivated to hold on to an unhealthy relationship she could not live with.

The imprint of guilt due to her fear of losing her parents' approval was the first unresolved loss issue. She needed to deal deeply with her own values and conscience before God. She was looking at Mom and Dad, not herself. Her abortion added to the guilt and loss issues. Her repeated sexual surrender to Lonnie made her lose even more self-respect. It was a vicious cycle. His refusal to love her kept her trapped.

When Jesus took her guilt for the abortion and sex, she was able to let go of the relationship and begin resolving her deeper issues of self-expectation and value. Codependency for Gayle was, in great part, rooted in her unresolved loss due to the abortion. Resolving the loss freed her to face the remaining codependent patterns.

This is how it frequently works. The loss will further empower an existing pattern or tendency. The imprint of the loss tends to fully solidify the codependency. Until the loss is resolved, the one-way relationship patterns remain stuck even though we know they are unhealthy. Gayle knew she was locked in an unhealthy relationship. The power to change came with the resolution of the loss.

Embracing Our Loss

The power to begin change in my one-way relationship began when I started dealing with the unresolved loss.

Resolving loss means coming to accept ourselves and others. It is like saying to God and ourselves, "I've lost and it's okay . . . something of value has come from the loss." That does not mean acceptance of the loss says we would have wished the loss right from the first. It means that loss is unavoidable in life. There is no way around it; it will come to all. It is what we do with the loss that counts. It can either be a stepping stone to greater security in God or a stumbling block to more defeat in our life. We alone can choose.

Loss therefore touches us at the deepest levels of our security and need. This is what makes it so difficult to accept. Everything in us wants to say *no! no! no!* A powerful law of relationship in loss says that whatever we have the hardest time losing is what we have the most need for. Whatever loss is left unresolved represents the key issues to be resolved in our lives.

Our losses merely provoke our weaknesses and neediness. I needed favor and approval long before I lost so much that year. The loss only solidified the pattern and further tested the need. I did not respond rightly. I did not work through my grief to resolution of my anger toward Dad and myself. My guilt over failure and my parents' separation and my fear of losing more were constant, gnawing companions. These all represented deep needs in me that should have been faced and resolved. I was too insecure and too guilt-ridden. I was the hero and caretaker in my family, wanting to save the family's reputation by being successful. I did not realize at the time how unhealthy it was. If I had dealt with the imprint of the loss, I could have been different and my relationships healthier.

If we embrace our loss and work through the grief with Jesus, we will come to acceptance and resolution. There is a scriptural law of the universe that states "How shall a man gain his life except he lose it?" The more we lose of ourselves and, by extension, our desire to do what we want when we want, the more of God we stand to gain. If we replace our deep need for people, places, and things with a foundational need for God first, then we will lead a healthy life. Each loss we suffer is an opportunity to invite Jesus deeper into our lives by making Him our security instead of what we lost.

The more you and I let go of our losses and come to acceptances, the healthier we become and the less codependent. Our only guarantee, however, of rightly resolving the loss is to invite Jesus into the place of need that the loss represents. God has promised to supply all our needs according to His riches in Christ Jesus.

When I finally cried my tears of loss and profoundly shared with Jesus my anger, fear, and guilt, I felt his acceptance. At first it felt strange to mourn something that had happened more than twenty years ago. But it worked. I felt the self-judgment, fear, and shame dissipate.

Many of us will need to walk through this process with Jesus more than once. For some it will even take another person helping. But it will work, and it does release us from the negative imprint if we are willing to look deeply and honestly at ourselves. He is more than able to bring change to our inner beings and, by extension, our relationships.

Here is a sample prayer you can pray to begin resolution of your loss with Jesus.

Dear Jesus, I offer to You today my heart of pain and grief over the loss of _____. The loss caused me deep pain because it represented a loss of _____ in my life. I need You, Lord Jesus, to comfort me with Your oil of joy for my mourning. Please take away the pain of my loss and replace it with the gift of Your felt love, acceptance, and forgiveness.

Forgive me for my contribution of _____. I turn from my judgment of others and myself. I vow to please You first, not myself or others.

Thank You for Your love and healing.

Amen.

Chapter 9

Most of us who love, care, or give
too much for the wrong reasons
have secrets—things we are
ashamed of. Codependency
and its patterns of
relating have everything to
do with our secrets and shame.

9 You're Only as Sick as Your Secrets and Shame

THE SAYING IS commonly shared in Alcoholics Anonymous groups: "You are only as sick as your secrets." I've added shame. You are only as sick as your secrets and shame.

Secrets and shame are the unrecognized cancers of our soul. Most of us who love, care, or give too much for the wrong reasons have secrets of which we are ashamed. Things we do not want to admit for fear of losing—losing the love, care, or admiration we so desperately need. We wonder if others will reject us or what they would say or think if they really knew us and our secrets.

We have different kinds of secrets: Things that we have done and don't want others to know about are the most common ones.

Tim had a secret he hid from Marilyn. Marilyn was pregnant with their first child. The discomfort and changes in her hormones made her more difficult to get along with. As Marilyn complained, Tim retaliated. He stayed later and later at the office, working on projects with his secretary. The inevitable happened. He had an affair with his secretary. It was short-lived. He felt guilty the entire time and was ashamed of himself. But he never told Marilyn.

Tim believed the often expressed sentiment "What you don't know won't hurt you." But this secret hurt their marriage. Tim's guilt perpetuated his dishonesty with Marilyn. He became less transparent and more afraid of her rejection. To please her, he told her what she wanted to hear, not what he really felt or thought. He also bought her expensive gifts, which made him feel better about himself and "made" Marilyn not be angry with him. His extravagance caused them financial problems, however, and Marilyn became confused and frustrated. "Why can't he just give me himself?" she questioned. "I want his time and attention, not things!"

Tim's secret reinforced the existing one-way relationship patterns and created even more problems in the marriage. Secrets cause dishonest patterns of relating, which reinforce codependency.

My attempts at helping them with their marriage problems had minimal success until a few years later. I saw Tim at a men's retreat, and he couldn't wait to tell me how much better his marriage was. The secret had been revealed.

"I feel so much better about Marilyn and our marriage because I feel better about myself," he explained.

"What happened?" I questioned.

"We had a horrible fight and Marilyn threatened to leave unless I changed. I told her I didn't want her to leave and had always been afraid she would leave me, especially if she knew the truth about me. We talked as we had never talked before. I told her the truth about my affair and my fear of her rejection. She accepted it, and it's been like a honeymoon ever since!" I congratulated him on his new-found honesty, thinking once again how powerful secrets can be.

Hidden or repressed secrets are especially powerful. The traumatic or hurtful events of the past can be so painful that we lock them away from our conscious mind. Memories of sexual molestation or abuse during our childhood frequently become secrets we hide in our subconscious. Sally's repressed memories of being molested had contributed significantly to her one-way style of relating. When the secret memory was revealed, the power of her codependency waned. The secret carried great shame, which fueled her codependency.

Family secrets breed shame. Alice had an uncle who was an alcoholic, but the family never talked about it or allowed Alice to say anything. The unspoken family rule was

"We do not tell." As a result, Alice felt ashamed. Children from alcoholic families are usually riddled with shame. A mother who tries to keep the father's drinking a secret experiences shame and passes it on to her children.

Shame-riddled families handle the truth dishonestly. Other, more subtle behaviors can enforce the "don't-tell" rule. Minimizing how bad the situation is conceals the full truth. And generalizing about the problem, skipping over the shameful details, also represses the truth.

Perhaps the greatest secret we keep relates to who we are. Bill is a very nice guy, who is also a sexual addict. He's been working hard on changing his life and has not visited prostitutes or porno shops for over a year. His addiction was a desperate attempt at getting love through sex. After a year had passed, I asked him how he was feeling about his addiction.

"The temptation is not there for prostitutes. I feel I have changed a lot, but I still have a problem."

"What still bothers you?" I queried.

His face turned red and his eyes shifted from me to the floor.

"I'm ashamed of who I am. I'm afraid of letting anyone know what I really am like on the inside. Especially the bad parts. I've always felt this way but have never told anyone before."

Bill's embarrassment eased as we spoke. I understood his shame. His secret is really a fear we all share. At the heart of all secrets is the fear of exposure and the consequences. If others really knew what we were like, would they still accept or love us? The truth about ourselves is the "Big Secret" in all our lives and often relates to the shame we carry and our desperate need to release it by sharing it with others.

Shame is the enemy within. It is the painful emotion of embarrassment about who we are and what we've done. We feel naked and exposed when we feel shame. We feel woefully vulnerable and fear the consequence. Once we feel shame enough, it becomes an inner state of existence. It becomes a fact, not just a feeling.

Shame is at the root of our codependency. It causes distorted self-worth, which then causes us to love, care, or give for the wrong reason. We do it all to make ourselves feel better about ourselves. Anyone who is loving, giving, or caring too much for the wrong reasons is responding to a damaged sense of self-worth—loving to be loved because of feeling unlovable; giving to receive because of feeling unworthy to receive; caring to cover feelings of not being valuable enough to be cared for.

Shame leads us to a state of self-rejection making us feel unworthy and unlovable because we are so painfully embarrassed about who we are and what we have done or have not done. Shame energizes and pushes us to self-doubt, self-consciousness, and low self-esteem. We do not value ourselves rightly. We are made to wallow in our inadequacies.

The classic codependent is often described as a fearful doormat, who feels responsible for everything. Guilt-ridden, the codependent believes everything would be all right if only he or she could change or do something different. Such a person is trapped by self-judgment, self-rejection, and low self-worth.

But there are also angry codependents, who are not doormats. Instead, they insist on their rights and demand that others change for them. They feel victimized by the other person's lack of love, responsibility, or caring. They demand because they feel the other person is wrong and they are right. This is really a mask for not having to be vulnerable and ask for love. It is safer to say "You're not loving me" than it is to say "I need your love." At the heart of the demands is a need for love. They feel unlovable but don't want to admit it. It is easier for them to blame. But their codependency is also rooted in deep feelings of insecurity and low self-worth. They just have a different style.

Most codependents in one-way patterns or relationships are doormats at times and angry at times. They switch from blaming themselves to blaming others. Either way the root of codependency is tied to shame and distorted self-worth.

Codependency affects us all, and at the very heart is

a distorted perception of self. Shame fuels this distortion. Shame causes us to keep the secrets. The shame and secrets both cause us to doubt our value to God, self, and others. It is a vicious cycle of hiddenness and self-defeat.

Self-worth is tricky. How much should we value ourselves? Is there a right way to value and a wrong way? What about the Christian concept of dying to self? How do you have healthy self-esteem and die to yourself at the same time?

While no one says to feel bad about yourself, the plethora of books on how to love yourself better or how to have a better self-image only confuses the issue. Some self-proclaimed gurus on the self say, "If it feels good, do it," or "Take care of yourself. Trust your inner self. Find your true self. Find the real you," or "Take these twelve steps to a better self-image."

I am concerned about all this advice about "self." It can help in the wrong way. For many it only helps them to become happier through being more selfish and self-centered. It does not make them better givers or more unconditional lovers. Too often they mirror the other nongiving or self-centered person in the relationship.

The truth of the matter is that few of us really know what to do with the "self." We either pamper ourselves or revile who we are. We either defend "self" at all costs or feel we should have no "self" at all. We humans have a basic inability to come to peace with ourselves and others. We are overcome with the notion of self-discovery, assuming that the more we know of ourselves the better we will be. But self-discovery for its own sake is dangerous. We run the risk of becoming only more enlightened, self-focused persons.

Self-Recovery

I believe the true purpose of self-discovery is self-recovery, meaning recovery from a self-led, self-focused, self-absorbed life. This does not mean we should be other-led, other-focused, or other-absorbed with people, places, or things. Dealing rightly with self means becoming God-centered and God-focused. To do so rightly requires self-discovery. It also requires an absence of self-judgment and hate. Self-judgment and hate put us at war with ourselves. They make us self-focused, overcontrolled, and jealous of others. And it further requires a recognition and release from self-love. We all want to comfort and pamper ourselves, which only leads to more self-centeredness and ultimately being controlled by our appetites.

When our goal is to become God-centered, then our ability to deal with both our self-hatred and self-love is vastly improved. We cannot trust ourselves, but we can trust ourselves to God. We do not have to be so uptight about not being perfect. The sickness in all of us is too much self-focus for whatever reason.

Self-discovery is good when it does not become the obsession of our lives. It should be a by-product of trying to live rightly, not a goal in itself.

By now you are aware that many codependents who love, care, or give too much for the wrong reasons suffer both self-hatred and self-love. The self-hatred can come from past love deficiencies and the self-love from our attempt to find a remedy. No one ever loves perfectly unless God motivates the loving. Our lack is a lack of godly love, even more than human love. The tendency to be codependent comes from our human nature and is in all of us to some degree. Simply repackaging our lives with the latest self-help series does not help our hurts. It takes a spiritual awakening in Jesus Christ to resolve it fully. He offers us a brand-new nature. Joy and peace can then become an inside job.

The self-hatred and self-love are greatly fueled by our secrets and shame. Some react to the shame by boasting and denying that it hurts.

In grade school my cousin had a reputation for not being bothered by paddlings. Whenever students behaved badly in the classroom, they were taken out to the inner courtyard and spanked where everyone in all the classes could hear the swats and the poor kid's crying. It was more embarrassing than hurtful. But my cousin never cried; he laughed instead. It was his way of defending against the shame and not giving in. He refused to be shamed. But I wonder if in refusing the shame, he also refused the truth of his own misdeeds.

A common reaction to wrongdoing is to deny that one is wrong. This keeps us from feeling the shame. My wife had great difficulty admitting to wrongdoing in areas of our relationship until she faced her shame. Being raised with much shame can cause a child to vow not to see the truth in order to avoid facing the painful feeling of shame. Families that are critical or status-conscious breed shame. They will overtly or covertly send the message "Don't shame us by doing wrong."

This can cause denial, rebellion, appeasement, or deceit. The child, not wanting to risk disappointing parents and feeling the shame, will deny any wrongdoing or rebel and defiantly say the rules are wrong. In fact, the rules are usually wrong and right: right in principle but usually wrong in motive. Shame-bound rules may sound like good ideas but are established for the wrong reason. They are to please others and promote image rather than health. Rebellious kids from good families are frequently reacting to the shame that goes with the rules.

Children who do not rebel in shame-oriented families become people-pleasers. They try to do everything to please Mom or Dad and make everyone happy so that they don't have to risk the disappointment and shame. Or they lie a lot to cover up their inadequacies.

Fearing his mother's rejection and disapproval whenever he did not meet her expectations, Neil began lying. He knew she didn't like rock music, so rather than tell her his band was playing rock music, he lied. He did not want the anger and disappointment. He ended up lying about everything that his mom faced him with. It was as though he felt inwardly he could never meet her expectations and lied to keep away the disappointment. He felt ashamed of himself when he disappointed Mom. He also felt ashamed of his lying. It became a self-defeating cycle of deceit and shame. He dealt with his girlfriend the same way, never being honest because he feared her rejection. He promised her anything but made excuses and lied when he could not measure up. The shame that began in his family fueled his codependent patterns in relationships everywhere.

When authority figures or parents put great pressure on a child for performance, shame results. Discipline with comments like these breed shame:

"Shame on you."

"What is the matter with you?"

"You are stupid" or "You're a dumbbell."

"You can't do anything right."

"You make me ashamed to be your mother/father."

"I don't know what to do with you."

Having a parent, child, or family member who is out of control, impaired, or retarded can bring feelings of shame. Ana's mom was mentally ill. She did crazy things such as stripping naked and walking outside into traffic. This shamed Ana deeply. The neighborhood boys teased her about her "crazy" mom. Embarrassed by other people's reactions to our loved ones, we feel the shame for them. Being teased also adds to shame. I was a freckled-faced redhead in adolescence. Kids incessantly teased me about my red hair. It embarrassed me and made me feel different, feeding the enemy of shame within.

But it does not have to be this obvious for a child to feel shame. Children have a great need to feel accepted and included. Any family difference of religion or culture, even an eccentricity, can breed shame in a child if it is not openly, caringly, and honestly discussed. Shame grows in the darkness of denial and concealment. It diminishes in the light of acceptance and honesty.

Children take on shame very easily because of their lack of psychological defense. The more vulnerable or impressionable you are, the greater the potential for shame. Sensitive children are easily shamed. Vulnerable moments can also be powerfully shaming. My wife has a vivid memory of one such incident during her teenage years. She and a friend had been stopped by the police and taken to jail for drinking. Her dad was called to come and get her. Being in jail was a terrifying experience. When her dad came, she ran to him for safety. Instead, he pushed her away and bawled her out in front of everyone. The shame was powerful because she felt so vulnerable.

But the biggest potential for shame comes from abuse and sexual defilement. The powerlessness against abuse and the vulnerability of sexual violation make shame an instant by-product. Mentally, emotionally, or physically abused children conclude there is something wrong with them, either totally or in part; otherwise they would not need the abuse they get. They blame themselves and yet feel violated at the same time. This compounds the shame message of "I'm bad," "I'm deficient," or "I'm the problem."

Bill's dad beat him severely with his fists and kicked him all the while, saying, "If you would just behave yourself, I would not have to do this."

Bill hated the beatings, resented his father, and yet felt he was to blame. He told me in a session, "If I hadn't disobeyed, Dad would not have had to beat me."

This erroneous belief caused him to see himself as bad and at fault in all situations. When his wife was unfaithful, as she frequently was, he saw it as his fault and took on her shame. He deserved it for not being "good enough to her."

Abuse works this way. It confuses what is right or wrong in the one abused. Sexual abuse is especially damaging. Teasing young girls about their bustlines causes shame. Wrong touching, rape, incest, or even pressured sex makes the recipient feel tainted and ashamed. If the sexual defilement is imposed from an early age, the abused persons will accept the responsibility for the shame and invite codependency by being too responsible, too caring, too loving, and too self-effacing for all the wrong reasons. Out of shame, they will feel it is their fault, that they are not good enough, that they are to blame.

Sexual defilement and abuse are at the root of a great

many codependent patterns and require special attention and focus. If you have been defiled or abused, do not take it lightly. Face the incident and work through it until all the shame is gone. Find a qualified member of the clergy or a Christ-centered professional counselor to help you sort the truth from the lies and pray for healing. It can make a significant difference in how you deal with yourself and others.

It took an unusual experience for me to face my shame and become healthy. It does not have to work that way. You can begin today by following these steps. Consider each one in prayer. Do not rush. Let the shame and secrets be exposed and dealt with. Shame is the enemy within that must be exposed and released in order to deal rightly with ourselves and others. Don't hold on to secrets and shame. Get rid of them all. Now!

Step 1

Recognize and recall your shame and secrets. What are you most ashamed of? What don't you want others to know about you or your past? Make a decision to face your shame by admitting it to yourself. Shame begins to go as we admit to ourselves that we are ashamed, that we do have secrets. Do not be afraid any more. Face it so that it can leave.

Step 2

Make a decision to turn your shame, your secrets, and your past over to Jesus. You cannot handle it all by yourself. You need His help and caring. He can and will forgive anything you ask of Him. If you confess your faults, He is faithful to forgive you and cleanse you from all shame. He can also release the shame you feel from what others have done to you. Trust Him. He is faithful. You cannot do it alone.

Step 3

Confess all your shame and secrets to God and to someone you can trust. Remember, there always is someone who can be trusted: A pastor, priest, counselor, or good friend can always be found. The willingness on your part to take the step of confession will begin to release the tormenting fear of exposure.

Step 4

Uncover the roots of your shame. Most shame comes from the things others have done to us or against us, as well as mistakes and sins we have committed. Accept responsibility for your wrongdoing, but do not accept responsibility for what others have done to you or against you. Especially do not believe the damaging lies others have told you about yourself. Admit and uncover these and take whatever steps are necessary to bring healing. Follow the steps outlined in the chapter on how to heal your wounds. If you are shame-oriented, look at how your family used shame to control.

Step 5

When the situation is right, admit openly those things that were shameful to you. The open sharing of my shameful past has helped me see that I am not perfect and that it is okay. Neither my past nor your past has to control the present unless we let it. Shame carries with it a fear of rejection and more shame. Push through the fear. Risk it. Ask Jesus for His strength. It will help.

Step 6

When appropriate, make amends to those you have cheated, offended, or sinned against. For some, restitution and reconciliation will be needed to resolve the shame. Get counsel on how to do it, when to do it, and with whom. A clear conscience has no shame.

Secrets need to be exposed and shame cleansed. Loving, caring, or giving too much for the wrong reasons can be empowered by the secrets and shame. Release comes as we face our fears of exposure and risk. We are imprisoned only by our own fear, not by other people's acceptance. We are only as sick as our secrets and shame.

Chapter 10

We all have been wounded and brokenhearted at times. We can recall some event or time in our lives when we felt a deep wound of spirit. Our inner being felt pained and pierced to the depths. The wound was powerful and hurt us deeply. Wounds are like that. Like outer physical wounds, inner ones can cause damage. Wounds and bruises can be on the inside just like the outside. The inner ones are not always visible, but they are there and affect our lives. Some things are hard to see but terrifying to feel.

10 A Wounded Heart's Cry for Love

THE LIGHTS WERE LOW, and every eye was riveted on the stage. She gave him a come-hither smile and pointed to his heart. She wanted it. He hesitated. She snuggled closer and played with his curly hair.

He couldn't resist. He melted like wax, took out his heart, and placed it in her hands. She smiled with glee and the audience applauded. He was overjoyed. He'd done it. He'd given her his heart and she had fully received it.

The scene changed. She was now playing with his heart. She tossed it up into the air. He gasped, but she caught it. The audience laughed nervously. She did it again, higher this time. He scrambled for it. Too late. It shattered on the floor. The room went quiet. He was in despair and she gave a sheepish grin. He knelt by his heart. Sadness filled the room as he picked up the pieces.

The heart was mended and the relationship reconciled, but no one was laughing when the lights came on. The scene had been especially poignant. It touched us all deeply. It made me and, I think, all of us recall how painful broken hearts can be.

We have all been wounded and brokenhearted at some time in our lives. We can all recall some event or time in our lives when we felt a deep wound of spirit. Our inner being felt pained and pierced to the depths. We hurt, we cried, maybe even felt the pain in our chests. The wound was powerful and hurt us deeply. Wounds are like that, some more and some less powerful, but all hurtful. Like outer physical wounds, inner ones cause damage. Wounds and bruises can be on the inside just like the outside. The inner ones are not always visible, but they are there and they affect our lives. They can even cause death.

Inner Wounds

I live close to a very large retirement community. It is common to see many of the elderly residents die. It is also common to have the spouse die shortly thereafter. I've heard the family say, "Dad just gave up. He didn't want to live anymore after Mom died."

They recognized the power a deep loss can have. A piercing inner wound can kill the will to live. Once the heart is wounded and the desire to live gone, death comes more quickly. Our inner being, spirit, or heart (Scripture uses the words interchangeably) is the seat of our deepest affections and desires. It's from our inner being that the issues of life flow. Our spirit motivates, guides, and empowers our life. A broken or wounded spirit is unbearable. Unless the wound is healed properly, our inner being remains damaged, and our resolve to live rightly is weakened.

Suicide comes from unhealed inner wounds. It is an outer act of destruction caused by an inner devastation. Many are so wounded inside that they feel suicide is the only way out. They have given little pieces of themselves away so often that suicide becomes an easy escape, for they feel there is little or nothing left inside to kill.

Unhealed or scarred-over inner wounds are the powerful hidden reasons for all self-defeating, self-destructive patterns in our lives. They are the hidden power behind our codependent patterns of relating. They are also the cause of many other maladies.

An associate of mine made a list of problems that can indicate unhealed or scarred-over wounds.

Depression

This common problem usually has a physical contributing factor, but the unresolved wound of loss is invariably associated with depression. Loss of self-worth, significance, acceptance, or belonging precipitates the depression.

Depressed individuals need to face their wounds of loss and their wounds of rejection. The anger and self-pity of depression are usually connected to a perceived rejection by someone.

Many individuals suffering from depression are more truly codependent. The depression is a symptom of their unresolved relational disappointments. Codependent people experience depression because they are trying to regain love lost or never given as well as deal with the rejection and low self-esteem they feel.

Recurring Painful Memories

Most wounds of life are retained as painful memories. When the pain of the memory is gone, the wound is healed. Recurring painful memories indicate an unhealed wound. Remembering the event, circumstance, or relationship without pain is the goal. Trying to forget only scars over the wound. I remember how deeply rejected I felt by my first love, but as I reexamined the relationship and prayed, the pain left and the wound healed. Codependents have vivid and painful recollections of past loves and rejections. These wounds need healing.

Inexplicable Inner Pain and Conflict

Deep feelings of pain, anguish, or inner turmoil usually indicate that something important is unresolved. When these feelings last or recur, the problem is usually a wound of the past needing recognition and healing. There are reasons for why we feel as we do. Most of them will have to do with repressed painful and wounding events of the past. If we try only to ignore or forget the pain, the wound will not heal.

Stuck in or Glued to the Past

Ever know someone who cannot let go of the past? They still think about old loves, experiences, or events frequently. That is usually an indication of an unresolved hurt. The wound is crying out for attention, and we are responding by remaining stuck to the event or memory. Wounds of loss, when unresolved, can cause this. Codependents are stuck in and to the past. We have trouble letting go of both the good and bad parts of the past that are interfering with current relationships.

Romanticism

I remember a movie in which Natalie Wood tried to re-capture a lost teenage love. It didn't work, and the movie closed with a poem written by William Wordsworth. It started with "Gone are the days of splendor in the grass" and closed with the question "Is it better to have loved and lost, than never to have loved at all?" The lines and movie evoked deep feelings of nostalgia and sadness in me for years after. They were romantic reminders of a lost teenage love. The memories dripped of nostalgia until my teenage love wounds were healed.

Sad, romantic memories are really unhealed wounds. Nostalgia is often an unresolved loss. Codependent romantics try to recapture past romantic memories or ideas in the present and it doesn't work.

Compelling Quest for That Which Was Unreachable in Childhood

I know of a man who hoards food. He never had enough to eat as a child and now has to have more food than is needed to feel secure. He has seriously considered buying a grocery store, but his wife absolutely refuses to give in to his obsession. The wound of his childhood deprivation is not healed, and he feels compelled to make up for it.

Codependency is a lot like this. It is a compelling quest for the lost love of childhood. It's a wounded heart's cry for love. It is an attempt to make up for what was never given in childhood or was lost after it was given. Healing of wounds is necessary for codependents.

Overemphasis on Sex

Sexual obsession or abuse can be due in part to a wound of the past. In men the obsession for sex, pornography, or masturbation can be tied to a feeling or fact of being cheated. The feeling of being cheated out of something is a powerful motivator for overemphasizing a need. A past wound of sexual infidelity or promised sexual pleasure that was never fulfilled can produce a desire to gain that which was lost or promised and never given. The result is called concupiscence or inordinate sexual desire.

It can work the same for a woman wherein sex is her attempt to heal the wound of sexual or emotional rejection. Trying to recapture that which was lost or never given always leads to overemphasis and obsession. Codependents are usually obsessed with their need for sex or love because of past wounds.

Low Self-Esteem

This common plague is almost totally due to the unhealed wounds of the past. My self-inflicted wounds, as well as the wounds inflicted by others, have damaged my self-worth. Until I faced the wounds of loss and shame, I was unable to free myself of the negative self-judgments that are a foundation to low self-worth.

Codependency is not caring rightly for ourselves, all the while trying to care for and about everyone else. We take responsibility for everyone and anything but rarely for our own need to be healed and fulfilled.

Out-of-Control Emotions

The Scripture says, "He who is slow to anger is better than the mighty, / And he who rules his spirit than he who takes a city" (Prov. 16:32). Self-control and therefore the rule of one's own self are to be desired. Most people who do not rule their spirits have unhealed wounds of spirit. The wounds need healing, the scars removing before self-control can be established.

These inner wounds are just like outer wounds. Touch a sore finger, and you will instinctively draw back. Touch an inner sore, and your emotions will react out of control. Codependents are out of control in the areas of deepest wounding.

When the wounds are healed, the control can be exercised. Before that, it will be difficult to have emotional control and do what is right. The strong emotions will hinder our ability to control ourselves. Codependents have difficulty controlling their emotions.

Feelings of Loneliness, Abandonment, or Rejection

Everyone has these feelings at some time in life. However, when recurrent or overpowering, they can signify unhealed wounds. Marilyn always felt lonely until she realized how often she was left alone in her room to lick her wounds and keep out of sight. Mom was abusive, and her dad advised hiding out.

Recalling the memories led to healing the wounds and security in Jesus. Before this she sought solace in the arms of men. Codependency is a wounded little girl's cry for love.

High Need for Attention, Approval, and Acceptance

These are all signs of unmet or wrongly met needs in the person's past. Unmet or wrongly met needs create wounds deep within us. I remember meeting a little boy who grabbed me by the leg and would not let go. He was starved for love and attention. His mom was disgusted with his desperate display. It shamed her and seemed to make her reject him all the more. It made him need the love more. A wound of love surely started the problem, and his mother's continuing rejection peeled off the scab before the wound could heal.

Any desperate need for affection, attention, or approval speaks to an unmet need and unhealed wound. Codependents need attention, approval, or affection too much. The unhealed wounds of the past continue to fuel today's codependency.

Addiction to Love, Relationships, Men, or Women

An overemphasis on any of the above is what codependency is all about. We put too much emphasis on our own needs and give too much power to the object of desire. Our unhealed wounds of love empower our need to be loved, cared for, or respected too much.

Let me emphasize again, codependence is a wounded heart's cry for love. It is the symptom of a damaged inner being, a broken heart, a wounded spirit. The codependent's inner being has been wounded and damaged by life. We are trying desperately to heal our broken hearts with a one-way relationship. And while the love, affection, and attention of relationship help soothe the wound temporarily, these rarely heal the wound permanently. The codependent continues to love, care, and give too much for the wrong reasons. The other person continues to take more than is given. The codependent ends up wounded again.

Sally is a case in point. Her life illustrates how deep and damaging to relationships the unhealed wounds in life can be.

Sally's dad was an absent father, a salesman, who was gone much of the time. When he was home, he drank and fought with Sally's mom. Dad never seemed to have time for Sally. He was always busy or gone. He was also critical of her behavior. Sally vividly remembers her four- or five-year-old self rushing to greet him after a long absence and being told as she was pushed away, "Don't hang on me. You're messing up my shirt."

She retreated in pain and confusion thinking, "Doesn't Dad love me? What am I doing wrong?"

Her father's rejection hurt. It caused a deep inner wound. The wound scabbed over but was reopened so frequently by his critical words that it never healed properly. It left a scar.

Her mom gave her attention only when Sally listened to the problems with Dad. Sally's wound caused her to draw close to Mom for whatever affection and attention she could get. The wounds from Mom's hurtful marriage found solace in Sally. Mom became more daughter than parent. She received comfort from Sally rather than giving it.

Following a fight, Mom would share with Sally all of the negative and hurtful things Sally's dad had done. Sally felt sorry for her mother, who always said, "It's okay. All I need to do is love him more and take care of him better and things will be okay. You don't know how hard things have been for your dad."

Sally began to think like Mom. Poor Dad. She also made excuses for him and saw herself as the reason he did not give her the attention she needed. She thought, like Mom, "If only I am nice and more careful with Dad, he will be nicer to me." It did not work.

When there is a deficit in love, attention, or approval for a child, the child usually accepts the fault, excusing the parent. Sally thought something was the matter with her. Her wound caused her to take on the blame. She judged against herself and vowed to do whatever was necessary to get Dad's attention and, by extension, the attention of other men.

As Sally grew up she put a lot of time and effort into her dress and her mannerisms. Boys noticed her when she was all dressed up. She wanted their attention. Because she was pretty and flirtatious she got the attention she wanted. But they gave it in order to get the sex her seductive ways promised. She ended up giving sex in order to keep their attention. This pattern continued, causing her to choose men who were attracted to her seductivity instead of her character. This pattern set her up for relational failures.

Her wounds were not healed. The scars of the past were controlling the present. She was reacting to the present as though it were the past.

Sally and I dealt with each of the areas of her life through discussion and prayer. Change came, and the chains of codependency no longer held her in bonds. She was free.

The healing prompted Sally to spend time with her own daughter, Kathy, and explore the effect of her codependency on Kathy, a cute fifteen-year-old girl, who did not date and emphatically didn't want to date. She, like Sally, had not had fatherly love, acceptance, or attention. Her father never called, and her stepfather never cared. She had been Sally's confidante and fully realized what both men had done to her mom. This made Kathy resentful of men, also fearful of them. Her love wound caused her to judge against both of them and vow to herself never to need a man.

The wounds of her family and upbringing caused her to distance herself from relationship. The resultant scar caused her to harden her heart against men. She will have difficulty becoming intimate with a man. She will probably choose a man who gives, cares, and loves more than she does because this is the only way she can trust him. She will probably marry a man who is codependent.

When a person's heart is hardened as a result of the wounds in life, the love of those closest is severely tested. The other must give and give to prove love. At the least hint of the giving being stopped, the hardened heart withdraws, rejecting first to ensure that it is not rejected. Or it gives just enough to keep the codependent coming back. It is self-protective and does not want the risk a healthy relationship demands.

This is frequently how the other person in the one-way relationship ends up not loving, not caring, or not giving enough. The wounds and resultant scars have made them bitter. They are afraid to risk. They do not want to be hurt, so they have decided not to risk ever being wounded again. They want to be invulnerable to hurt. It is hard to love or be loved rightly when the wounds of the past are unhealed today.

Sally is working with her daughter on these issues. Kathy is starting to recognize and deal with her wounds. If she continues in her healing, she will be able to make healthy choices and break the pattern of codependency and judgment that has been in her family for generations.

Sally's wounds and those of her daughter are common to many of us. It is also usual that the wounds are not recognized and healed until they cause so much pain or so many problems that something must be done. Very few of us deal with wounds rightly. Too many times we think the only person who needs healing is the one whose wounds are visible, still raw, and tender to the touch. Everyone can see that help and healing are desperately needed. But these walking wounded are in the minority.

Most wounded keep it from showing, afraid to face the pain or let others see the wound. They become prisoners of their secrets. These inner wounds have scabbed over, not fully healed. New hurts come along, ripping off the scabs, keeping the wounds open and sensitive. Sally got rejected over and over again by her dad. The sting of the latest rejection had not worn off before another was added. Marriage problems are frequently this way. The old sores get touched on over and over again, never getting a chance to heal. The person keeps reacting out of the unhealed wound.

However, the ones that scar over can be the most dangerous. Scar tissue is not as resilient and pliable as healthy tissue. A person may think the wound is fully healed and not realize that it is wrongly healed, leaving a hardness or brittleness. A decision not to love again, not to risk, or not to care is what scar tissue is all about. It is self-destructive healing. If scar tissue forms, the wounded area will never function fully and perfectly again. It will be damaged by the wrong inner responses we've made as a result of the wound.

Vows and judgments are the raw material of scars. When we judge against ourselves, God, or others, because of our wounds, then scar tissue forms. When we vow or pledge never to love or risk again, scar tissue forms. When we become bitter or fearful of being wounded again, scar tissue forms, and the sore is wrongly healed.

Codependents fit all three of these scenarios. They can be the walking wounded, with scabbed-over, unhealed wounds.

Our inner wounds come from the rejections and sins of others against us. They also come from the losses of life and ways we are shamed through wrongdoing. Sally's rejection by both Dad and Mom were reinforced by her losses of love, which added to the pain, and her desperate responses added to the shame. Rejection is a big issue for all codependents. We all have to face it at some time. People who suffer from codependency seem to be more sensitive to rejection than others. They also are less able to resolve rejection issues. I have been very sensitive to rejection and rejection issues. The sensitivity has served me well in counseling but has caused me distress in personal relationships. I very easily sense other people's approval or disapproval of me. I can easily tell whether or not they agree or disagree with something I have said and whether they receive or reject me. It is as if I have a built-in sensor that continually registers distance or closeness in relationships. It also registers the relationship tension, affection, and approval or lack thereof. Individuals who have codependency in their lives have these sensitivities.

Some rejection is obvious—when a person tells you of his or her dislike or pays absolutely no attention to you or will not talk to you. Most rejection, however, is not so obvious. It is covert rather than overt. It is the kind of rejection that is hard to acknowledge immediately.

Betty's overprotection, worry, concern, and fear for her daughter were forms of rejection. I later spoke to the daughter, who confided that she felt she could never live up to her mother's expectations. She didn't feel confident. She felt inadequate because Mom was always there telling her a better way to do something or a different way. Mom kept saying be careful; look out; don't hurt yourself. This made the younger woman second-guess herself. A subtle form of rejection, it caused her to reject herself. It caused her to choose men who used her because she believed any flattery she was told. She sought out men who purposely gave her a lot of approval and attention to build her lacking self-worth. They were usually the kind of men who wanted something from her. They wanted sex. They wanted her money. They wanted a lot of things, but they didn't really want her.

Rejection works this way. It eats at our self-confidence. It causes inner doubts and self-judgments. It makes us choose paths and relationships that do not work. Rejection produces a neediness for the approval and acceptance that was not provided. Many carry this wound and seek the approval, attention, and acceptance they so desperately need. This again is codependency.

Others, however, scar over the wound and deny their need. It is their way of dealing with the hurt of rejection. They say they do not need love, attention, approval, or acceptance. They remain aloof and distant. Or if they are in a relationship, they remain only for a short period of time. They cannot stand to be vulnerable very long. These are the people codependents usually marry, those who are wounded also but may have dealt with their wounds differently.

Wounds are powerful motivators for relationship. Most wounds in life are relational wounds. Rejection is a relational issue. The wounds of rejection in the past determine the patterns of relationship in the present. Codependency is a rejected person's attempt to deal with rejection.

There are hidden rejections that we often do not think of as rejections that affect our codependency. Being an unplanned child, being illegitimate, and even being a daughter when a son was wanted (or vice versa) are all forms of rejection that a child can sense deep within the spirit. There are individuals who have survived being aborted, who are attempting to prove their right to live, attempting to get others to accept them. Being a replacement for a lost child is also a form of rejection. You will always try to make up to your parents and to others for what was lost. You will be afraid of disappointing others. Codependency is trying to replace or regain that which someone else lost so that you have a place of acceptance for yourself. Codependency is trying too hard not to disappoint others.

Review your early years. Was your father or mother absent very often? Did you end up in the nursery or with baby-sitters a lot? Were you ever held, breastfed, given attention or affection? If you were not, there are probably roots of rejection that go all the way back to your early years. How your parents disciplined you will also affect your feelings of acceptance or rejection.

Some parents have difficulty with their own anger, and they raise children with anger or even abuse. Other parents are impatient or critical. All these lead to a deep inner response in a child that says, "Something is the matter with me"; "I must be bad"; or "I am not adequate." And the child spends a lifetime trying to win people's love, to feel adequate and okay. Other children will become bitter from this same rejection. They will have angers or hostilities of their own. They will have bitter roots deep within them because of the abuse, because of the punishment, the criticism, the anger they have suffered. They can become the abusers of the future. They can become the angry spouses of the codependents. They can become the hostile abusers who have dealt with their hurt or wound in a different way.

Maybe your family was different. Maybe there was no anger or abuse in your family, but there was perfectionism. There was a lot of emphasis on rules. The rules became more important than you. Children raised in these families end up feeling they don't count or they don't measure up. They are always trying to prove themselves to other people, trying to accomplish things to get others' approval, love, attention, or acceptance. They become performance oriented and people-pleasers.

Some, however, decide they can never measure up, and they go the other way. They seem to never accomplish anything. They purposely rebel and say, "I don't care about the rules; they don't apply to me." They become self-centered and make their own rules. They are also the ones codependents often marry because they seem to be in control. They know what they are doing, and the codependent seeks so much to have the security, the approval, and the affection of somebody to make them okay.

Maybe your family members were neglectful, just not there. They did not take care of you. They were absent or uninvolved in your life. That would make it hard to grow up and feel you were important to anyone. Instead, you think, "I don't count." You may have problems with intimacy because you want to count so much that you will do everything you can to make sure that someone else thinks you matter. Or you may take the other path, the path of hardness that says if you do not pay attention to me and make me count all the time, I won't give you anything. These are the wounded souls codependents often marry. They are hardened; they are hurt; they do not know how to love.

There are other examples of rejection that can affect our lives: an unfaithful spouse; a rejecting boyfriend or girlfriend; an unwanted divorce; being fired from a job—all of these deeply wound our inner being and cause us to make choices and develop patterns of relationship that do not work. Healing requires facing the wounds of rejection that feed our codependency. Wounds need healing, not hiding.

Chapter 11

Healing wounds requires a
willingness to face the painful
event or memories of the
past. We need to give God
and ourselves permission
to unlock the doors of memory.

11 How to Heal Your Wounds

HE TIGHTENED THE SCREWS holding her shaved head and put the electrodes in place. As the tiny bit of electricity touched parts of her brain, she vividly relived the memory. She once again saw her mother standing on the porch waving good-bye. She smelled the lilacs in bloom and felt sad.

This original piece of research in brain activity demonstrated how every experience in life is recalled in our brain as memories and mental images. Individuals with near-death experiences frequently tell that their whole lives seemed to pass in front of their eyes when they were faced with death. The memories of life are recorded in our brain permanently unless the brain cell dies or is damaged. What we saw, smelled, touched, tasted, and felt is all recorded in the memory.

The wounds of life are imprinted as memories and mental images. The painful feelings associated with the memories need to be released for the wound to be healed. Our memory of what we saw, smelled, touched, or tasted will usually remain the same. But the negative feeling associated with the event needs to change. This is the basis of all inner healing. Additionally, our inner judgments and vows regarding that event also need to be reexamined and changed.

Healing wounds requires a willingness to face the painful event or memories of the past. We need to give God and ourselves permission to unlock the doors of memory. The problems of the present are fueled with the unfaced pain of the past. Hiding the pain continues the problem. Revealing the memory brings healing. Ask God to show you the hidden or forgotten hurtful memories that are still empowering present problems. Codependency is a rejected person's vain attempt to fix the rejection and pain. The wounds affect us and empower the way we relate to others. Look for those contributing wounds from the past. If necessary, write out a personal history. Spend time writing what you know about the chronology of events from before your birth through adulthood. Be as specific as possible. Any image or impression is valid. Take special note of things that were important to you as a child, memories that stand out. Look for the pain in them as well as the gain. Especially look for events that may have caused you to devalue yourself or others seriously. Have you made inner vows about yourself such as "I will never be like Dad (Mom)"; "I will never trust men"; "I will never raise my kids that way"; "Just wait until I am older; I'll do it right"; or "Something is the matter with me; I'll never do it right"?

Pain empowers each of these vows. Look for that pain. It needs healing, and the vow needs changing. The vow may have helped for a moment, but it was not helpful over time.

The pain of loss is equaled only by the pains of rejection and shame. Codependents need healing from the wounds of loss, shame, disappointments, and rejection. Codependent patterns of loving, caring, and giving are vain attempts to avoid rejection and try to regain what was lost in order to heal the wound. Or the patterns are used to avoid similar circumstances in the future so as not to get hurt again.

When facing these wounds, be careful to distinguish your own sin and wrong responses from others' sins and offenses against you. Codependents have made inner responses to other people's wrongdoing. The rejections of childhood and the wrong patterns of family need fulfillment have caused wrong inner judgments and vows.

As you begin to remember painful memories or realize hurtful influences in your past, do not minimize or discount them. Every painful memory is important; every unhealed wound needs healing. Face each one.

Do not make excuses for those who have rejected or wounded you. Parents are imperfect. All parents hurt their children. Some do it wittingly and even maliciously. Most do not. Most parents do it inadvertently. They are preoccupied with their own lives and problems. Their wounding of you was an outgrowth of their own sin and sickness. You need to see how your family, your parents, your brothers, sisters, grandparents, uncles, aunts, or cousins wounded you. Did they meet your basic needs for love, attention, affection, affiliation, acceptance, ability, and affirmation? If not, they probably sinned against you. Were they critical, neglectful, or shameful? How did they hurt you and wound you? Who else has hurt you?

"It's not her fault!" Joey screamed. "She did the best she could. Raising nine of us kids was not easy." The anger and rage was evident in his clenched fist and glaring eyes. Joey was not willing to face how Grandma had hurt him. She had taken all nine kids in after Joey's mom had abandoned them.

"But Joey, Grandma beat you and locked you in the closet for hours," I pointed out.

"It doesn't matter. I deserved it. I was a bad kid."

Joey was stuck in his anger and rage because he could not admit that Grandma had done wrong.

Healing of wounds requires identifying those individuals who have wounded you and honestly dealing with how they hurt your inner being. Again, do not make excuses for them. Healing and resolving do not come when we minimize, rationalize, or excuse what really happened.

Grandma really had beaten, abused, and damaged Joey. He was unable to come to healing for his own rage and codependence until he fully faced and admitted what Grandma had done to him.

After seeing her sin against him, Joey was now faced with the most crucial issue of all healing. Would he be able to forgive Grandma for what she had done? Any wound of life is almost impossible to overcome unless forgiveness oils the path to change. In my past there were many wounds, and much forgiveness was needed. I was faced with forgiving my parents for the marriage problems that caused the breakup of my family. I needed to forgive my dad for his conditional love and violent temper. I even needed to ask my dad's forgiveness for siding with my mom when I could not really know what was between them. I needed forgiveness for the resentment and bitterness I carried.

All forgiveness is really healing of the past. It is a letting go and letting God be God. It is a profound recognition of everyone's wrongdoing to us and even our own wrongdoing to everyone. It is an acceptance of our humanness coupled with a decision not to allow the sin and sickness to win. As we forgive we let go of the pain, let go of the wrongdoing, accept the outcome, and go on with life.

But the kind of forgiveness I am talking about is not the kind that pretends. Real forgiveness is for real wounds that really occurred. Pretending only stuffs the problem and the pain, cursing us to relive the consequences. True forgiveness is choosing to forget in spite of remembering.

Forgiveness does not wait for the other person to change. There is no demand in forgiveness. There is only release. Forgiveness is unconditional. It is a giving up of one's rights. In forgiveness we recognize what was unfair but still give up the debt that is owed. We become willing to give up our own defenses. We do not blame others for what we have done. We release them and ourselves. Vivian Stewart from Oklahoma City, Oklahoma, writes:

Release

I weep and wash the day away, the day, but not the hurt
   away.
The sharp-edged thoughts of yesterday seem even more
   acute today.
Is there no killer for the pain? Will jagged memories ever
   reign to conquer each tomorrow?

And in the throb of sleepless night, I sense a star of
   warmest light showing me the only way.
Forgive. Forgive the hurt away. Or it will haunt and taunt
   and stay. Forgive.
Forgive the hurt away.

The true and healing kind of forgiveness is a rare gift we
give others and ourselves. It is a giving up of our rights, our
defenses, our self-righteousness, and our hurts. It is a promise
to ourselves and to others not to bring up the offense again to
them, to others about them, or even to our own thoughts.
True forgiveness is a true letting go of the past. Forgiveness is
the only release for bitterness, resentment, and wounds. For
some the wound is so deep that forgiveness will require God's
help. Jesus was able to forgive those about Him who hurt
Him so deeply. Ask Him to give you that same power to forgive others as He showed on the cross.

But some will say, "I have forgiven, but the pain is still
there and the resentments come back. Isn't forgiveness a
choice?"

Corrie Ten Boom was a prisoner of war incarcerated in
a German concentration camp during World War II. She suffered atrocities and saw her family painfully abused. Walking
down a city street in postwar Germany, she encountered the
familiar face of a German guard at her concentration camp.
Her heart sped up and the anger rose within. He passed on
the other side of the street, and the emotion subsided. She
wondered why she was still angry. Had she not forgiven? She
had prayed to forgive.

She went immediately to visit her pastor. After sharing
her dilemma with him, she followed him to the bell tower,
where he had her ring the large tower bells with the bellrope.
The bells rang a loud ding-dong, ding-dong, ding-dong. He
then told her to stop pulling the rope. The bells continued to
ring ding-dong, ding-dong, ding-dong until they slowed into
silence.

Her decision to forgive was a releasing of the bellrope of

resentment she had pulled on for so long. There were a few ding-dongs left after the decision was made.

This is the way it will work for most of us who have been deeply wounded by others. We need to face fully the wrongdoing against us, to make a decision to forgive, and work toward the day when the residual ringing stops.

Jesus can empower the decision and even quiet the clanging, but only we can choose to forgive. We need to let go and let God take over our injustice, pain, and resentments. The sound may reverberate and the hurt not immediately cease, but the freedom, the release, the love that returns is so precious and needed.

To fully empower your forgiveness, follow these simple prayer steps.

Share with Jesus all your pain, shame, and disappointment. Relive your painful memories or mental images with Him in prayer. Be rigorously honest. Tell Him how others have wounded, hurt, and sinned against you. Don't hold back. Nothing is too small or too petty. Get it all out. The tears, the anger, the resentment, and the secrets.

Tell Him you release to Him the right to judge them for their actions or lack of action. Give them to Him. Ask Him to deal with them and their sins. Tell Him you choose to forgive and release them of their debts to you. You will no longer carry the guilt, shame, or stain of their sin or wrongdoing against you.

Ask Him to cleanse you of your inner response and wrong subsequent actions to their sins against you. Ask Him to forgive you. Offer up to Him your wrong inner judgments and self-defeating vows, the ones you made against yourself and others because of the pain. Ask Him to break their power over your life.

Thank Him for His help and forgiveness. Believe He has heard your heartfelt prayer and realize something will begin to change in you.

This kind of prayer has led many to healing. When the wounds are healed we make better choices, choices that are healthy and not self-defeating. The codependency of today is empowered by the wounds of the past. Freedom from the pain gives us new life, new hope, and the ability to love rightly.

Chapter 12

Mishandled anger is hurtful and destructive to people and relationships. It is another breeding ground for the codependency in us all. Winning is a release from the control anger has over our lives.

12 How to Face Their Anger and Win

IT IS HARD for us to deal with anger. Our own or the anger of others is a powerful emotion. Codependents especially have problems with anger. Most were raised in angry homes, have married an angry spouse, and don't know what to do with personal anger or somebody else's anger. Verbally or physically abusive persons are angry. They explode their anger all over others. It comes out in fits of rage: cursing, name-calling, violent outbursts, even physical beatings. This type of anger is similar to a tornado that blows through town, leaving a path of destruction and bewilderment in its wake. It can come unexpectedly, do its damage, and leave quickly.

My family was like this. I have been this way. I exploded with angry accusations and cursing, then was over it in five minutes. I had gotten all my anger out and felt good again. But my wife, Susan, was reeling emotionally from my outburst. She came from a family where anger was expressed differently. Her family never yelled, screamed, or lost tempers. They handled their anger primarily through silence and withdrawal. This second major type of anger is called passive-aggressive anger. It is a way of being angry and even punitive without being outwardly aggressive. Susan would withdraw and become noncommunicative even up to a week after our encounters. Angered by the withdrawal, I would explode again. She added on three more days of retribution. Our vicious cycle continued until we both started realizing how destructive anger can be.

Mishandled anger is hurtful and destructive. It causes

deep inner wounds. It can be intimidating to others. It is especially so for children.

A sharp-tongued, critical parent deeply wounds the spirit of a child. A violent, abusive, or rage-prone parent wounds the inner being of the child. A passive-aggressive parent accomplishes the same thing through the silent rejection of withdrawal. These expressions of anger all add up to pain for a child, who then becomes frightened of triggering the angry reaction, tiptoeing around Dad or Mom to avoid setting off the anger or causing the withdrawal. They also try to please so that Mom or Dad will not be mad or criticize them. This starts a codependent pattern in the child, who will love, care, or give in order to avoid the anger, loving for the wrong reasons.

I did that in my family. My dad had a violent temper and was verbally and physically abusive when angry. I remember tiptoeing around Dad, not wanting to get too close in case he was angry. I was always testing the water to see if everything was all right. I did not want to be hurt again by the anger. I became fearful and a people-pleaser, but other kids become rebellious, defiant, and angry in return. Their wounds cause them to strike back and defy or rebel instead of retreat. They become bitter and angry at the injustice of it all. My brother, Larry, used to be like this. He was angry and explosive. It was also hard for him to let go of his anger. His wound had caused him to become like our father. This is one way the sins of the fathers get passed on to the children even to the third and fourth generations.

My dad's father was an angry man. He ran a bar in a rough-and-tumble mining town. My dad tells the story of how my grandfather would bring a shotgun to the dinner table, threatening all twelve kids with the gun unless they were orderly and quiet.

My grandfather's anger was passed on through his son to me. Even though I was scared of anger, I still got angry the only way I knew how—through rage. Knowing how hurtful this anger was to others, I felt guilty and ashamed immediately after an outburst, which made me swing too far to the other end of the spectrum. I promised Susan anything just to keep her from being angry with me so that I wouldn't feel guilty. I became the model husband. But when she remained angry and withdrawn for days at a time, I once again swung back the other way and exploded.

Rageaholics are like this. They can be the nicest people you would ever meet. They will do anything for you. They'll even go out of their way to bless you. But look out! If you cross them too much, they will swing back the other way and let you have it. They'll even write you out of their lives. They know no middle ground. It is all or nothing. This pattern becomes so established in their lives they become proud of it and boast how they are either "all for you or will have nothing to do with you."

Rageaholics make a lot of relational vows and judgments based upon their own unhealed wounds. They justify their actions. In families with a rageaholic father or mother, the nonraging spouse and children take responsibility for the rageaholic's anger. They say to each other, "Well, you asked for it. You should have known better than to do it. You should have known it would make Dad (Mom) mad!"

The rageaholic's angry outbursts are always accusatory. Since anger is self-justifying, rageaholics will always make their anger the result of someone else's behavior. They will blame you for making them angry. They will say, "It's all your fault . . . don't make me angry and everything will be okay." This is damaging, creating self-doubt and causing the spouse to live in fear and codependency.

It is especially damaging to children who believe the raging parent's accusation that it is all their fault. It will cause them to take responsibility for other people's anger but rarely their own. They become confused as to who is really responsible for the anger.

I felt guilty after my angry outbursts but did not take full responsibility for my anger. A part of me still believed that it really was Susan's fault that I got so angry. Yet I also knew such anger wasn't right. I was confused about my anger and that of other people. I blamed myself for Susan's anger while thinking at the same time she was also responsible. The ambivalence and confusion kept me stuck in my anger and made me tiptoe around other people to avoid precipitating their anger. This is codependency. It is a mixed motivation for loving, caring, and giving. Am I really loving to keep the anger from biting me? Or am I loving in order to bless the other person and make his or her life better?

Anger is usually tied to abuse. Anger is a powerful emotion. It is the power behind the abuse. That is why rape is considered an act of violence rather than desire. If others have been angry, controlling, or critical of you, you may have been abused.

Abuse is both subjective and objective. What is abuse to one may not be for another. There are also differing levels of abuse. There are powerfully abusive codependent situations and there are mildly abusive ones. Either way, abuse is an issue we all must face. We all have the potential for being abusive and probably have been abused in some way. Understanding abuse is important to healing codependency. Most codependents come from a background of dysfunction and abuse. Most female codependents have been, like Sally, sexually abused at some point in their lives. This has come through date rape, molestation, incest, or unwanted sexual pleasure. Many codependent men come from physically or verbally abusive homes.

Abusive parents or spousal anger causes a lack of healthy self-acceptance. The child or spouse will internalize the anger and abuse that goes with it, believing in great part what the anger and abuse are saying: "Something is the matter with you, or I would not have gotten angry!" This message is conveyed in a powerfully imprinting way. The anger and abuse are so intense, so dramatic, and so powerful that it convinces the child or spouse that a defect exists and causes the anger.

This is probably the most destructive result of unbridled anger from rageaholics, passive-aggressive individuals, or critical people. It seriously wounds a person's self-concept. It causes the person to rage inwardly. It creates an enemy within that constantly undermines confidence, self-esteem, or value in life. The person whose spirit is damaged will have great difficulty finding and embracing a role in God's plan.

The unbridled anger or abuse of a parent creates codependency in the kids. The unbridled anger or abuse of a spouse provokes codependency in the marriage. The anger and abuse wound, hurt, confuse, and threaten. The loved ones of angry or abusive people need a lot of inner healing.

Wendy's story reveals how one codependent woman struggled with and overcame the fear of her husband's powerful anger and abuse. It's a tribute to her courage and God's faithfulness:

> I was afraid of his anger. I would do anything to avoid it. He was verbally abusive, called me names, and threatened me. He would also punish me. I called it punishment because he got mad at me and then withdrew. He would not speak to me or members of the family for long periods of time—even up to two or three weeks.
>
> I couldn't stand it when he didn't speak to me. I was always afraid he would get mad, curse me out, and then close me out. I was afraid so I would lie about things that could trigger his anger. I lied about spending money because it was a hot issue in our house. I did it all the time because I could not endure the consequences of his anger.
>
> My husband and I were not Christians when we married. It was a second marriage for both of us. The divorces had not been pretty, and we both sought solace in each other's arms.
>
> Our backgrounds were a big part of the problem. Earl is a recovering alcoholic, and my mom is a practicing alcoholic. Earl was delivered from the compulsion to drink through watching a fellow on Christian television. Along with the alcoholism had also come an alcoholic personality of anger and abuse. Earl had quit drinking but hadn't dealt with these underlying character defects.
>
> My fear of his anger was also coupled with the fear he would leave me. He enhanced the fear by continually threatening to leave. I lived in constant torment of the fear. Becoming a Christian helped me, but it didn't resolve our problem and my fear. That is, not until the day I decided to change.

We had another fight, and Earl was verbally abusive to me. I cowered in fear. Earl finished his tirade and walked out of the room, refusing to talk to me. I hated his withdrawal because I hated how it made me feel and act.

I begged him, "Don't be angry with me. I'll do anything to make you happy. I'll do anything you want." All I got in return were more angry looks and silence. I was so desperate, yet ashamed. I was sick of being tormented and begging forgiveness. I decided to talk to my pastor, hoping it would help. He listened carefully, then asked, "Have you ever stepped back and looked at Earl when he was angry?"

I said, "Of course not. I'm too afraid. His anger paralyzes me."

He encouraged me to realize that all the anger coming from Earl was not for me and it wasn't even all from Earl. He told me to step back from the situation the next time Earl got mad and look at how angry he got. I was not to take the anger personally. He reminded me that "we wrestle not against flesh and blood" and that I should not wrestle with Earl over the anger.

I felt more hopeful returning home. It made sense. I knew all that anger in him wasn't just him.

The next time he got angry we were traveling in the car. I started to panic as he exploded, but I stopped reacting and began to laugh. His face was red, and he was spitting as he cursed.

"Earl, you're so angry," I said. "Look in the mirror— you're even spitting."

He was befuddled for the moment, then continued in his anger. But I was different. I had stood back and looked at him as my pastor had suggested. I did not take on all his anger. I didn't believe it was all directed toward me. I didn't let it pull me down and beat on me. It was great. I wasn't as afraid as I had been, and Earl even looked funny.

The incident made me realize how my fear was a factor in allowing his abusive behavior. Not that his anger was my fault, but my fear of the anger was contributing to the problem and was supporting the wrong pattern. I saw how our home and marriage was full of my fear and his anger. I was afraid; he got angry. He got angry; I got afraid. The fear fed the anger, and the anger fed the fear. It was a vicious cycle.

Someone asked me which came first. I said I didn't

know, but since Earl was older, his anger must have been first!

I was now getting healthier but still hadn't faced the fear of his leaving me. This changed when I got a sponsor for my overeating problem. She asked, "What is your biggest fear?"

I always said, "Earl leaving me."

She would respond, "Isn't God sufficient in your life?"

I answered, "I don't think so, but I want Him to be."

Finally it dawned on me that God was sufficient to take care of me if Earl left. In the middle of a nasty fight Earl said, "I'm leaving."

I heard myself say without hesitation, "If you choose to leave, I can't stop you." It took the wind out of his sail. He never threatened again. The power of that fear broke in me and between us.

But the biggest challenge was yet to come. We joined a twelve-step Christ-centered program called New Wine. The group scared me to death. The group leaders, Joe and Betty Moore, spoke of honesty and confrontation being necessary for change. Betty was especially confrontive. She said, "Don't sugar-coat sin. Confront it and call it what it is."

Reluctantly I began to agree with this approach to honesty. I became willing to speak up to others about Earl's shortcomings and my fears. We committed to meeting with Joe and Betty as couples. The hot issues of our marriage surfaced, but it was okay. This was a safe way to begin change. Soon we committed to meeting with a group of other people.

I told Earl openly for the first time that I was not going to let his anger control me again. I wasn't going to beg and plead with him not to be mad with me anymore.

My stand was soon tested. We fought over an insignificant issue, and once again he blasted me. I took the issue to the group for discussion, but Earl was angry and getting angrier.

"I don't care if I hurt you or not," he said. "I'm not sorry for what I did, and I'm not going to apologize." He had moved into his stubborn stance and refused to listen to the group or me. He withdrew again and moved into the other bedroom. The silence began. I hated it. The punishment was horrible. I began to pray and called the group for support. They encouraged me. During one of my prayer times, I also felt God's encouragement. The inner voice seemed to say, "This is going to be a long siege, but it will break the stronghold." I counted on this promise many times in the days to come. Every time I felt desperate, I prayed or called a group member for support. I knew this was a spiritual battle and I wasn't supposed to rescue or fix Earl. I had to be strong and wait for God to do it.

A week went by with no change. Two weeks went by, and it was time for our group to meet again. He refused to go, so I went alone. I was so mad! How could he be so stubborn? I wanted to kick down his bedroom door and beat him to a pulp.

I was angry and knew it—so angry that I asked the group if I could leave home for the weekend. I was scared of what I might do if I stayed. I went to another couple's home for the weekend but didn't tell Earl where I was. Sunday came and I needed to get clothes for church. I knew Earl would be gone, so I got in the car with my friend to go. But I couldn't do it. Something rose up in me so strongly I couldn't budge. I couldn't face going back to the house. I was petrified. My friend comforted me and went by herself to get my clothes.

Monday came and it was time for me to return home. Earl would be at work and I could be safe at home. I got ready to go, and again this fear rose up in me. It was so strong I felt paralyzed. I couldn't move. I couldn't go home.

I had dealt with my fears but never saw myself as deeply fearful, but as I stood there I realized how fearful I really was. I had been fearful even as a child. I never knew what shape my alcoholic mom would be in when I came home from school. Getting off the bus, I waited for a car to come, then ran as fast as I could. If I beat the car home, I imagined Mom wouldn't be drunk. If I didn't, she would be.

The fear had been there from the beginning. It pushed me and made me play silly games. It was my attempt to overcome the pain of coming home to a drunken mother. It also made me do many other things. It was what drove me to be codependent. All my life I tried to shape things up, fix people, rescue others, or make sure every situation worked out. I wanted everything to be okay. I knew the fear had to go. I had invited it into my life and now had to renounce it. I prayed with my friend. I repented of my fear, renounced it, and instantly felt freed. It was gone and I knew it. I was different.

I returned home without fear. Earl came out of his withdrawal and noticed I was different. Others also remarked, "You're really different. What happened?" I also noticed other changes in myself. I've always been afraid of the rides at Disneyland. They were scary and I didn't like them. I went back to Disneyland after my change and found I was not afraid any more. I enjoyed the rides. The fear was gone from many areas of my life.

We're still in a commitment group, and I'm free from the bondage of fear in my life. My refusal to contribute to the sick codependent pattern has also caused Earl to deal more with himself and his anger. We are both doing better and are grateful for the change.

Wendy's story has all the right ingredients for learning how to face someone's anger and win. Winning, in this sense, means being able to handle the other person's anger effectively and in a manner that doesn't destroy you. Anger is a powerful self-justifying emotion. It can wound deeply if not rightly managed. The Scripture says, "Be angry and sin not." This admonition recognizes the fact of anger in our lives but cautions us on how we use it.

Learning to Respond

Learning how to respond to someone else's mismanagement of anger is a must for everyone. There are a lot of frustrated, angry, critical, and controlling people in this world. Learning a healthy response to them will protect us from deeper wounding and encourage problem resolution instead of personal assault and character assassination and abuse.

The following steps are important considerations for anyone facing an angry, critical, controlling, or abusive person. Study them thoughtfully.

If the Person Is Physically Abusive, Get Help and Get Away as Soon as You Can

Don't challenge or provoke a physically abusive person. The person is dangerous and out of control. Biblical submission does not include physical abuse. Physical abuse of you or others is against the law and life-threatening. It not only can kill or maim physically, but it creates deep inner bruises and wounds. Don't believe a physically abusive person's promise to not hurt you or others again unless you know the person has been healed. A promise or change of heart is not a healing. Healing requires a deep inner dealing with the roots of the abusiveness. A willingness to look at the roots of anger and hurt and be accountable to others is the truest indication of real change.

Do not trust your own evaluation of the change. Let a qualified pastor or counselor evaluate before you recommit to living in the same house. On the other hand, realize that abusers can change. Give them the opportunity to prove it before writing them out of your life. God changes things *and* people.

If the Person Is Sexually Abusive, Get Help

If the person has abused children or others, do not shield and hide the wrongdoing. In most states it is unlawful not to report sexual child abuse. The abuser will continue the pattern until something drastic happens. It usually takes a crisis to shake the abuser from the denial and force change. Don't be afraid of creating that crisis.

If the person abusing you sexually is your spouse, get help for yourself first. A qualified pastor or counselor will guide you on what steps to take. Marriage is not a covenant of abuse.

Abuse of any form needs to be quickly uncovered and dealt with. It is not an act of disloyalty to do so but rather a healthy step toward resolution.

If the Person Is Verbally Abusive, Don't Tolerate the Abuse by Listening to It

Listening to the words will only wound, hurt, and tear you down. It can also provoke your weaknesses and cause you to do things that make the problem worse. Excuse yourself from the situation. When the person is no longer angry or abusive, share with him or her your willingness to work out the problems, but emphasize your refusal to be dumped on. The abuser may not appreciate your stance at first, but over time it will reduce the insanity and out-of-control emotions.

Deal with Your Own Anger

Anger is contagious. The wrong response to someone else's anger is to give in to yours. It is natural and understandable that you may become angry. But look at what the anger is telling you about yourself and the situation. Anger is a self-justifying or self-preserving emotion. Your anger can be highlighting a need in you that you have not seen or a facet of your character in need of change. Admit to your anger and find out why it's there. Angry reactions, especially those that end up out of control, are usually triggered by something in the present that resembles the past. Much of our anger is due to past unresolved issues. Anger is like water accumulating behind a dam. With additional rainfall it can overflow and create an unexpected torrent, destroying everything in its path.

I frequently overflowed my dam because I stuffed so much unresolved offense behind it. Don't stuff your feelings. Get them out and resolve them or they will burst the dam.

Face Your Fear

Fear is really negative faith. It is the worry of things that rarely come to pass. Fear is faith in your enemy rather than God. It is scary to deal with an angry person. But realize that most of the fear is coming from your unfaced wounds of the past. Fear will rob you of any potential for change. The only way to overcome your fear is to admit it and look to where it came from and what it's about. Make a decision not to let the fear rule you or keep you from doing what's right. It's the fear that has you captive, not the person's anger. Pray and ask God for help with your fears. Also do as Wendy did. Get someone else to support you and tell you the truth. Fear is always a piece of truth mixed in with a lie.

Don't Let Self-Pity Grab Hold of You

It hurts to be blasted, criticized, or abused by someone. When we are wounded by others, our desire is for comfort and relief from the pain. However, chronically focusing on how others have wounded us can turn into the snare of self-pity. If we nurse and rehearse the pain for the benefit of our own comfort, self-pity will reign. It will become the excuse for not getting up and going on with life. For some, self-pity can eventually lead to self-punishment through punishing others. It is the power behind victims and martyrs.

Face your self-pity. Admit to it. Realize that self-pity can be a mask for not rightly facing your own anger at others and yourself. Face them with your anger and rightly admit to whatever you've done wrong. The self-pity will break.

Get Honest with Yourself and Them

Get over your fears, anger, and self-pity, and plan a time to sit and communicate. Choose a safe place and time and openly share your feelings. A good place for an event of communication like this can be a restaurant or a prearranged meeting with friends, a pastor, or a counselor, who can help keep it under control.

Be honest with how anger affects you. Use "I" statements such as "I feel scared when you're angry" instead of "you" statements like "You make me feel scared when you're angry." Share your thoughts and your feelings. Open up your heart. Don't hide or hurl accusations.

Listen

Ask questions about why so much anger is present. Use an interview style. Don't defend and don't respond to accusations. Instead, use this meeting as a fact-finding mission. See if you can get past the anger to see what's really in the person's heart. Take special note of any legitimate grievance which may be brought up. Angry people can still have feelings. Try to affirm and acknowledge nonangry feelings.

Do Not Take Responsibility for Another's Anger

Unbridled anger and wrongdoing are not your problems. Do what Wendy did, and try to depersonalize and detach from the brunt of the anger. Don't take it on. Don't listen to it. Don't let the power of it touch your inner being. Each person's anger is that person's responsibility to control. Out-of-control or vicious anger or criticism is not right, no matter what the offense. Realize your inability to prevent anger. You will not be able to be perfect enough to keep another from ever being angry. Don't try. The anger is there and will come out no matter what you do. Give back the responsibility for that anger.

Carefully Look at the Roots of Your Own Reactions to the Anger

Whether you become angry, fearful, or self-pitying, your reaction is probably fueled in part by unresolved issues in your past. Pray for God's revelation of these. As each incident comes, work through it with openness and prayer. The healing of your past will empower the present. It will enable you better to face today's anger. Wendy's recognition of her past fearfulness resulted in freedom from fear today. She was then able to face Earl's anger as never before—and win.

Set Boundaries

Carefully, through prayer and counsel, decide what you should accept and what you should refuse. Wendy realized her need to face Earl's threat of leaving by saying, "I can't keep you here; you can leave if you want to." This was her stand. It was her way of setting a boundary that Earl needed to face. She also set an important boundary for herself by stating to herself and Earl that she was no longer going to beg him not to be mad with her. Setting boundaries about what you can accept will bring sanity to the craziness. It is a way of doing what's right regardless of the consequence. It signals to the other person that you mean business. And it keeps you accountable.

Make Yourself Accountable

Accountability is a check and balance system that helps us to do what we say we need to do. Healthy accountability helps us do what is right, no matter what the cost. Wendy and Earl's change, in great part, came about because they joined an accountability support group. They went to others for help and it worked. We cannot do it alone. Deep, ingrained patterns of fear and anger will require the open honesty and support of others to overcome.

Each of these steps will better enable you to face anger and win. Face the anger, not only of the person, but of the past. I came from an angry home. I needed healing for the hurtful abuse of the past. Wendy needed a release from the fear in her past. Facing anger also requires facing the present. I had to learn how not to let Susan's passive brand of anger control me. Wendy needed to break the fearful control of Earl's anger over her life.

Winning is a release from the control other people's anger or abuse has over your life, both past and present. Winning is a freeing up of each of us to do what is right regardless of the cost. Winning is also a claim on self-respect because we're no longer reacting out of control. If you face the anger rightly, you'll win.

A treasured friend offers this meditation for all who have been wounded or abused:

> In the midst of my anger and pain, God tenderly speaks, "Fear not for *I am* with *you*."
> But God! Where have You been? I have been used and hurt and feel like a prisoner of my aloneness.
> "Be not dismayed, for *I am your God*."
> My God? How do I know You are my God?
> "By believing in Me. By trusting Me for your weakness. I will strengthen *you*. Don't let self-pity grab hold of you. Let the very personification of a holy God (I AM) meet your ultra-personal need. For I am with you always. *I* will uphold *you*."

Why, God?

"Because I have loved you before you were born. From everlasting to everlasting. I was and am and will be forever your God. Be honest! It is natural and understandable that you may be angry. Much of your anger is due to past unresolved issues. Face these issues. In My 'upholding you' your fear becomes faith. Fear is your enemy. Not God. Let Me keep one of my endless promises. '*I* will uphold *you* with *My* righteous right hand'" (Isa. 41:10).

God can do everything . . . but fail!

Chapter 13

The feeling of intimacy is
powerfully enriching.
Codependents cry out
for intimacy but rarely
achieve it until God heals.

13 Intimacy Can Cause or Cure Codependency

INTIMACY IS A commonly used word for an uncommon experience. Most talk about intimacy, but I wonder how many experience it. Intimacy comes from the Latin word *intimus,* meaning innermost. It is the profound experience of two or more individuals sharing their innermost beings with each other. It is the touching of two souls, the joining of two spirits. It's what everyone, especially a codependent, seems to want but rarely gets.

The feeling of intimacy is powerfully enriching. When we have a taste of intimacy, something in our inner being is affected. We are less alone, less pained, and seemingly more whole. The voice of the enemy within is quieted, and we feel deeply touched and inexplicably renewed. This is why intimacy is such a special experience. It can change you. Passion is the height of love, but intimacy is the depth.

Intimacy can also curse you. Codependents have difficulty with intimacy. They either seek it too much or avoid it. Or both.

I met Todd as he was completing his ninth treatment program for cocaine addiction. Only twenty-eight years old, he should have everything going for him. He is bright, insightful, articulate, and nice looking. But the cocaine has almost ruined him. Before leaving the program he shared an experience with a girlfriend the day before. She promised to meet him after work but never showed. This had happened before. Todd was hurt and angry.

We talked about the incident in group therapy. His codependent patterns came through more and more clearly. He said she always gave him mixed signals. The signals said both "come closer" and "stay away." He felt like a yo-yo. One moment she seemed to desire him; the next she was unavailable. He didn't know what to do. As he shared the story he got more and more upset, confessing to the group that he had even thought of taking her out into the woods and forcing her to stay with him there until she made up her mind to let him past the barriers and into her life.

We all suggested that she would definitely agree to do this while in the woods but change her mind after leaving.

He said, "I know! But I think I can get past her defenses and touch her deep inside. At least, she's told me I'm the only one who's really been able to do that to her."

The group countered with, "Her telling you that was just her way of keeping you hooked into coming back!"

Todd didn't like the feedback though part of him knew it was true. Todd is a cocaine addict, but he's also codependent. He's really searching for someone or something he can turn to that will touch *his* inner being as he wants to touch his girlfriend's. Todd is really seeking intimacy. He wants it so intensely that he's pressuring and even thinking of forcing her to experience it with him. This is another face of codependence.

Codependents want the intimacy because it touches at the deepest level of their inner being. It helps soothe the pains of low self-worth and the lack of love from childhood. It temporarily covers over our hurts and makes us feel valued and loved. It is like a drug to our spirit. It's what we have always missed and wanted. Intimacy stills the voice of the enemy within.

But it never seems to work for long. The other person withdraws or does not pursue any more.

We somehow fall through the cracks of relationships and receive less and less of the intimacy we so desperately desire. Soon we are loving, caring, or giving too much in order to be intimate. We end up having to pressure for it, like Todd, or earn it by going the extra mile and tiptoeing around issues that might rock the boat. We are afraid if we don't earn it, control it, or otherwise make it happen, it won't. We will even change our tactics and try to wait it out, testing to see if the other person will initiate the intimacy. When it isn't forthcoming, at least not by our timetable, we reaffirm to ourselves that we were right all along and as any good victim or martyr will do, we sacrificially give again in order to get. This self-defeating cycle can only get worse if we don't get better.

The codependent quest for love, affirmation, or attention is more truly a search for intimacy. The deep inner feelings of affirmation that are intrinsic to intimacy are what we all desire and lacked during childhood. Todd came from a broken family. His mother was an addict, his dad passive. Grandma and Grandpa were powerful family figures. Grandpa brought Todd close but also pushed him away through criticism and anger. Mom alternated between being drunk and sober. She too brought Todd close, then pushed him away. Todd never knew what it was like to be close and stay close. He chose women who said come close, then pushed him away.

He went through a period of choosing women who were clinging vines and wanted only to be close. But he didn't know how to handle their continual demands for closeness, so he would distance himself. When they became disinterested he again wooed them to draw close only to withdraw later and repeat the continuing cycle of codependency. It is a lonely inner cry for intimacy. The craving guarantees the defeat. The more one pressures for intimacy from another, the less it can occur. The more one seeks intimacy, the less of it one will experience. Pursuing intimacy is often, by definition, self-defeating.

Intimacy is not the goal of an ideal relationship but rather the by-product of a healthy relationship. It is a by-product of relating rightly to another. It is what results from setting our sights on relating rightly. Wounded hearts cry out for intimacy because the relationships of their lives were not healthy. They were not rightly related to with the honesty and transparency, caring and acceptance so needed for a healthy background. The intimacy was not there. No one was lovingly intimate with them. Or if it was present, it was distorted and attached to something in an unhealthy way. This is what can happen with sexual abuse. The sex gets confused with intimacy. And while sex is the physical act of intimacy, it is no guarantee of emotional and spiritual intercourse. Sex is the ultimate demonstration of intimacy, but it is not a substitute for intimacy. Intimacy is emotional and spiritual. It is experienced in our deepest inner being. Sex is to be the outward expression of that experience. Sex usually flows from intimacy, though it can also create intimacy. But we need to be careful not to substitute one for the other.

Sexual addicts are attempting to find intimacy through sex. They are wanting their deepest inner being touched. Sex has become ammunition for overcoming the enemy within. They are using sex to fulfill the unquenchable inner need that has not been met. As they engage in sex, they experience flavors of the real thing, but the taste only lasts for fleeting moments. They end up substituting sex, passion, and lust for love, affection, and intimacy. It goes the way of all addictions, progressing to destruction of the person's relationships and self because sex without emotional intimacy is an act that does not touch one's inner being.

Young men and women in our society are substituting sex for intimacy and are dissatisfied with the results. The substitution makes sex less than it is and intimacy more sought after than it should be.

Intimacy can work when it is rightly understood and the foundations of healthy relationships are practiced. The book of Genesis is often called the book of beginnings. In it is the story of Adam and Eve. After Adam was made, God said it was not good for him to be alone. Every beast of the field and bird of the air was surveyed to find Adam a helpmeet, or helping answer, but nothing was found. God caused a deep sleep to come over Adam, took a rib from his side, and created Eve. When Adam awakened and met Eve, he liked and accepted what God had done. The story, in free translation, goes on to say, "for this reason a man will leave his father and mother and cleave to his wife, and they shall become one flesh. The man and his wife were both naked and not ashamed."

The principles of this story offer insight into being rightfully related and intimate.

Aloneness is the root issue of intimacy. The problems of our childhood and life have left us feeling alone on the inside and alienated from ourselves. We fight the enemy within who does not validate or affirm us. We have trouble affirming, accepting, loving, and valuing ourselves. It is not good to be alone; we need others to join us in the affirmation and acceptance. If others don't accept us, it is difficult to feel accepted. We are social, relational beings. We need other people.

Marriage is going to be the most common but not the primary means of dealing with our aloneness. It is a helping answer to our aloneness and our relational need fulfillment. But notice that it is a helping answer, not *the* answer. The foundational answer for our aloneness is a relationship with God. People cannot fulfill deep spiritual or existential needs. Only God can. Abiding by this principle will allow people to meet the relational needs in a healthy way. Not dealing with fundamental aloneness through a spiritual awakening will put people in the place only God should hold. Intimacy with people works only when they hold this right place in life, where people and relationships are not our gods or our slaves. The rib came from Adam's side to denote equality and mutuality, not domination or passivity.

We need to leave before we can cleave. Simply, we have to let go of old relationships, especially with family and even ex-lovers, before we will be able to truly cleave to a spouse. Cleave means to be stuck together like glue. It takes this step of commitment to make marriage and intimacy work. Intimacy will not come about when the risk is too high. Commitment provides a safe environment for risk. Intimacy also cannot occur when old lovers haunt our memories. The past needs cleansing for the present to be freed up. Old wounds, dreams, and loves must be let go to give the current love a chance to grow.

Intimacy cannot be achieved when the results of our families' wrong patterns of intimate relating still control us. Todd's unhealthy family patterns of intimacy were still controlling him. He needed healing from their effect before he could learn to be intimate with others.

Becoming one flesh is the real goal, not intimacy. The unity of a one-flesh marriage is the goal to set our sights upon. As we learn how to come to unity and agreement, intimacy will flow. Unity is the right integration of the parts into a meaningful whole. It is not sameness. The challenge of marriage is unity of purpose, value, and direction. This will set the intimacy in motion.

Being "naked" is the first component of intimacy. "Naked" comes from the Hebrew word *arom,* meaning without clothes, totally bare, without pretense or defense. It speaks to the need for total transparency, a total baring of who we are, who we were, and who we want to be. Intimacy requires complete transparency. Intimacy requires total vulnerability. Intimacy requires a total baring of our thoughts, fears, motives, and desires.

This is the work of intimacy. This is why most are not intimate. Few are willing to risk sharing fully who they are and what they feel for fear of being wounded and rejected. Yet risking the wound is what helps heal the child within.

Intimacy is a decision to risk telling all. It takes a decision. It also takes time and care. We need commitment; we need safety; we need healing. It's hard to be transparent if we've never been. Or if we have been and were hurt, we will need healing as we learn to risk our deepest inner being with others.

Intimacy requires a lack of shame. "They were naked and not ashamed" establishes biblically the need for being accepted and not rejected when we do share ourselves so that we won't walk away ashamed. Sharing our inner being with another who does not accept it will shame us. It will make us feel defective or deformed. We will be embarrassed about who we are and never want to risk the transparency and vulnerability again.

Shame is a powerful enemy. It can cause us to hide from others and even ourselves. It can cause us to seek intimacy in all the wrong ways. We will love, care, or give to be intimate but never make it work. Some fight the shame feelings by being too open, too honest, and too vulnerable with too many.

Intimacy is special. It can help us heal, but it requires the right process. There is no instant intimacy. It takes time and effort. It also takes God.

My codependency began to change as I learned to be intimate with God and with people. I learned first to be intimate with God. After I received Christ into my life, I experienced continued problems in my marriage and career. Someone encouraged me to tell all to Jesus. As I did, the burdens lifted and I began to change. Intimacy with God follows the same process as intimacy in marriage. As I committed to live my life and began sharing more and more of myself in prayer, He shared more and more of His love, forgiveness, and acceptance. Prayer times became deep times of felt intimacy, love, affection, and affirmation. He became real to me. He spoke to me from within, and the words were always encouraging, loving, and precious. I cried many tears and felt His love many times. It did something for me deep within! I was healed from the inside out.

Our intimacy began to still the enemy within. My wounds surfaced and were healed. I felt cared for. I also felt "fathered." The needs my dad was unable to meet became reality in my relationship with father God.

I recalled Josh McDowell's words: "Christianity is not a set of beliefs. It is a relationship with Jesus Christ, the God of this universe."

I needed the love and I still experience the relationship. Intimacy is a by-product of my shared life with Him. It is also a by-product of a transparent life with my wife. It has taken effort and commitment, but it works wonderfully.

The mishandled or absent intimacy of one's past helps to

create codependency today. The intimacy of today can help to heal the codependency of the past by risking vulnerability with healthy people.

Examine the intimacy patterns of your family and past relationships. See where they were unhealthy or lacking. Look for your inner vows, judgments, or wounds. Examine and discuss them with someone else. Pray through each one. It will bring healing.

Begin risking transparency in small ways with safe people. Honesty with others about your own self-love, self-hatred, jealousies, fears, and insecurities is needed. It will release the shame and still the enemy within.

Don't push for intimacy. Let it happen naturally. Also don't avoid it because of your fear of being wounded. Risk it. If you're hurt again, you can heal.

Learn communication skills. They go a long way to helping achieve intimacy, which requires communication. Ask questions and share. Don't dominate or be too passive. Get in touch with your own feelings. Many are not intimate because they don't know how they truly feel and therefore can't share feelings. Feelings are essential to being intimate. Learn how you feel; then share with others.

Work on putting sex where it should be. Sex is a part of intimacy, not a substitute for it. It is a physical manifestation of emotional and spiritual intimacy. Look at how you have used sex in your life. Was it an outflow of intimacy or a substitute?

Pay careful attention to boundaries. Some have no boundaries and an "anything goes" attitude. Others are overly careful about what is propitious and what is not. Intimacy requires recognizing each other's boundaries or lack thereof and negotiating a mutually satisfactory plan of care that does not offend yet enriches both.

Don't expect intimacy when there is no mutuality. Intimacy requires mutual risk. If you attempt intimacy when your relationship is one-way, it will often shame you and cause a deeper pattern of codependency. One-way relationships most often lack intimacy until the other person is willing to risk.

Start with God. He will take all your problems and release your pain and shame. His love is unconditional. Share your inner self with Him. He does not reject. Believe that He loves you deeply. He does!

Chapter 14

Codependency begins in the climate of unresolved marriage problems. Kids respond and react to what happens between Mom and Dad. The kids are the thermometers of family life. Mom and Dad are the thermostats. The marriage relationship between Mom and Dad controls the climate of the home. The kids register the result.

How to Prevent Codependency

"EVERYONE I KNOW is codependent in some way. How are we going to reverse this curse? Is there any way to prevent codependency?"

It was a good question, and I told her I was not sure of the answer. The question came from one of the women attending a seminar on codependency. I thought of all the things that could help prevent codependency, but one stood above the rest: healthy marriages. I also recognized that a great percentage of children will never be the product of a healthy marriage or any marriage. Yet my promise remains steadfast and gives us all something to hope and work for and build upon. Marriage is the foundational relationship of family life. All other relationships take form after the marriage. This means family life is shaped and controlled by Mom and Dad and their relationship. If the marriage is healthy, the other relationships can be healthy. If the marriage is not working due to one or both partners' dysfunction, the rest of the family will feel the impact. The kids will respond in unhealthy ways. Family system research has given us a clear picture of how this happens. For example, if Mom and Dad have a lot of tension and conflict in their relationship, one of the children is sure to do things to help calm the troubled waters. I noticed this with our youngest daughter, Katie.

Susan and I were having a heated disagreement in my office behind closed doors. Every few minutes Katie knocked and wanted something. It was starting to get on my nerves until I realized it was her attempt to resolve our conflict.

Kids react and respond to what happens between Mom and Dad. They are the thermometers of family life. Mom and Dad are the thermostats. The marriage relationship between Mom and Dad controls the climate of a home. The kids register the result.

Codependency begins in the climate of unresolved marriage problems. When Mom and Dad do not deal rightly with each other's needs, they will not meet the children's needs in a healthy way. Need fulfillment is the raw material of codependency. Our need to love, care, or give too much came from how our needs for essentials such as love, care, affection, and acceptance were met in us. If the marriage relationship is not working well, the emotional and relational needs of the children are not being rightly met. This imprints wrong patterns of need fulfillment. The children carry these wrong inner imprints into their relationships with others, causing the unhealthiness to repeat itself generation to generation.

Codependency begins in the need fulfillment of family life. The health of the family is directly proportional to the health of the marriage. Preventing codependency requires a healthy marriage relationship. If the marriage relationship isn't working well, the other family relationships rarely work well.

Healthy marriages require effort and commitment. We've all heard the saying "It takes work to make a marriage work." Most marrieds soon realize this truism. But healthiness in marriage requires more than effort; it requires effort aimed in a prescribed direction.

Sociologists have described the post–World War II era as a time of social evolution, experimentation, and rapid change. Our prewar model of how marriages should work was tested and challenged, creating confusion as to what a healthy marriage should look like. To know how to be healthy in marriage requires a model to aim for. If there is no standard to be desired or aimed for, every person will craft a private marriage relationship. In great part, this is our dilemma. Most don't have a good model for marriage in their parents and therefore are unsure what a viable model of marriage can or should be.

Adopting a healthy model for marriage is the first step in preventing codependency. A model is an ideal or a replica of something. A healthy marriage model gives us an idea of what is desirable. It provides an ideal to look to, a goal to head toward. How we live out our marriages will then provide a model to our children of how to live their relationships. If our model is flawed, theirs is also likely to be lacking.

A Traditional Marriage

In the 1940s and 1950s the prevalent model of marriage our parents practiced is what has been called the "traditional" marriage. Not all marriages were this way, but most had this flavor. In this model of marriage, Dad was the head of the home and Mom was the heart. This translated to mean that whatever Dad said, went. It went, that is, unless Mom could persuade him differently. Dad worked hard, and Mom took care of the kids and the home. My parents and many of their friends were like this.

When we got testy or smart-alecky, as kids often do, my dad would declare, "As long as I'm paying the bills, you'll do what I say. If you want your own way, then start supporting yourself."

Even though he said it half-kiddingly, we all knew it was what he really believed. He saw his major role as provider for the family, and this entitled him to give the orders. He felt that as long as he provided for Mom and all of us, we should be happy.

My mom's role was also well delineated. As long as she raised the kids, took care of the house, and gave Dad sex, she was fulfilling her role.

This model of marriage provided clearly defined roles, but it had problems. The man in a traditional marriage relied too heavily upon leading his family by being "authoritarian."

202 —— One-Way Relationships

He saw himself as a "boss." He got his needs met through control, domination, or intimidation.

The woman in the traditional marriage role was often a doormat and behind-the-scenes manipulator. She got needs met through compliance and manipulation. My mom was always working behind the scenes with us kids to keep Dad happy. "Don't let your father know if you don't want to get in trouble" was a frequently given message.

This model of marriage created problems with equivalency, intimacy, honesty, parenting, and even abuse. The woman was not perceived as equal to the man in value. Intimacy did not work very well and there was a lack of open honesty among everyone in the family. Secrets were accepted, even encouraged, and shame was the result. This model of marriage also excluded Dad from taking responsibility to parent his children and meet his wife's emotional needs. It also encouraged Mom to love, care, or give too much for the wrong reasons. This is a setup for one-way relationship patterns. Mom will seek out others to fulfill her emotional needs, investing too much love, care, or concern into her children or others because of her marital disappointment.

Dad will feel cheated if Mom or the kids don't respect him. "After all," he says to himself, "look at how I've provided for them. I gave them a home and food on the table. What more do they want?" He'll have difficulty seeing his responsibility to love emotionally because he gives so much physically.

It can also be a setup for physical or emotional abuse. Dad will be prone to exert his authority in the wrong ways. Mom will feel powerless or even fearful of stopping him. The children and even Mom can end up physically abused and feeling unable to do anything about it.

The kids will have problems. Their rejection of the model of marriage they have lived with will lead to confusion about how marriage is to work. It can be especially difficult for those from a Christian background. They will believe that the man is to be the head of the house and the woman the helpmeet, but they won't be able to accept how they saw it lived out in their home. This will cause them to give up the belief of the man being the head, or they will remain confused and silent on the issue.

A Negotiated Marriage

The kids of parents from traditional marriages in the forties and fifties experimented with new models of marriage in the sixties and seventies. They wanted something different but were not sure of what it should be. One of the first experimentations was the "negotiated" marriage. In this model of marriage, the roles in the relationship were negotiated and mutually decided upon. There were no set standards or rigid expectations. Everything from housework to raising kids and supporting the family was up for negotiation. The woman, fearful of being used or taken advantage of, demanded equality and freedom so that she wouldn't repeat her mother's mistake by being a doormat. The man was willing to give the freedom to her in part because he didn't want to be like his father. This also freed him from full financial responsibility.

Some typical marriage vows included contracts stating that housekeeping duties would be shared, finances kept separate, and independence valued. It was a vain attempt to resolve the unhealed wounds of their own family lives. When independence and separation are too strongly emphasized, interdependence, intimacy, and stability are threatened. It was a conditional marriage wherein a commitment was conditional upon performance and each person's behavior too self-focused and self-preserving. It was an overreaction to the hurtful model of traditional marriage their parents had practiced. Few of these marriages lasted. Security and safety in each other was hard to find. The unhealed wounds and scarred-over areas of their own lives found no healing in this model.

A Reversed Marriage

The other experimental marriage model has been titled the "reversed" marriage. In this scenario, the boss and the doormat change gender. The man takes responsibility for himself and maybe his job, but not for her or the children. He is a combination of his dad and mom. He won't parent his children or care for his wife's emotional needs. He escapes into himself or his work and is passive in the relationship. Tim was passive at home, never helping Marilyn with housework or parenting.

Tim saw his role as providing for himself and his family's financial needs. He did not, however, ascribe as strongly to supporting the family as his dad had. Passive husbands like Tim see a wife as more able to contribute financially, and they willingly share the role of financial provider with her or even give it away to her.

Marilyn, on the other hand, has refused to be a doormat and now has control of the family. She directs the traffic. She gives most of the thought and energy to what should or shouldn't be done. She is not under Tim's control, but this has not solved her problems. She still has nearly total responsibility for the kids and home. She, like other women in a reversed marriage, seldom gets her emotional needs met. She has more responsibility with less payoff. Her role is different from her mom's, but still not fulfilling.

Intimacy does not work well in a reversed marriage. Tim is usually secretive or dishonest because he fears her criticism. He promises and placates to get Marilyn off his back but rarely changes. She ends up being victimized by her attempts at control through criticism and pressure. The kids, of course, will respond negatively to the marriage model because they do not see intimacy, unity, equality, peace, and need fulfillment in their parents. The kids will suffer the effects of their parents' marital dysfunction.

There is another serious consequence of the reversed, negotiated, and traditional marriage models—divorce! There has been more marital separation and divorce in the last forty years than in the previous four hundred. *Newsweek* magazine published the following statistics:

Year	Number of Marriages	Number of Divorces	Divorce/Marriage
1890	570,000	33,461	5%
1955	1,531,000	377,000	24%
1981	2,400,000	1,200,000	50%

The increase in divorce and family disintegration from 1890 to 1981 is phenomenal. Marriages and families cannot break up without significantly affecting all members of the family and their relationships. The divorcing parents make deep inner evaluations and vows in response to the divorce. These inner judgments and vows are rarely healthy ones. They come from fear, hurt, or bitterness. They usually reinforce existing negative patterns or create new ones. Few adults work through their hurt, pain, and loss to the point of healthy acceptance. Fewer sort out the blame issues rightly.

The children are especially victimized by the dysfunctional marriage and hurtful divorce. They rarely have the ability or opportunity to deal with the deep inner wounds, judgments, and vows brought about by their parents' problems and/or divorce. Judith Wallerstern and Joan Kelly have done extensive follow-up research on the effects of divorce or separation on children. Their study shows that divorce is hurtful to children. The children rarely resolve the loss. The majority continue to harbor the secret desire for Mom and Dad to get back together even ten years after the divorce.[1] The deep wound of divorce in children is powerful in determining future relationship decisions. The children will make unhealthy choices out of their unhealed wounds.

---

[1]Judith S. Wallerstern and Joan B. Kelly, *Surviving the Breakup: How Children and Parents Cope with Divorce*, New York: Basic Books, 1982.

A One-Flesh Marriage

There is a fourth model of marriage—the "one-flesh" marriage. Many have found healthy guidelines in it.

In the one-flesh model the roles in the relationship are not individually negotiated or created out of reaction to past unhealthy models. Rather, the roles of the man and woman are adopted out of conscience moved by God. When the man fulfills his role as he believes God desires and the woman also, the frame of reference for choosing a model is different. We are not choosing our model of marriage out of past wounds or preference but from studied effort and conviction.

In the one-flesh model of marriage the man is responsible for more than the physical needs of his family. He also sees his role as helping to meet the emotional and spiritual needs of his wife and children. He is neither passive doormat nor dictatorial leader. He is a sacrificial leader who provides direction through example, encouragement, and problem-solving *with* his wife.

The woman sees her role as being coequally responsible for the emotional, physical, and spiritual needs of the family. She is neither doormat nor the one in control.

A one-flesh marriage is best described as a team of two gifted, mature, and committed individuals who desire God's direction and provision for their life and family. The husband is the team leader or managing partner. This does not make him better or more responsible than the wife. Both are equally responsible for their roles before God. She is the co-founder and working partner in the relationship. She does not take on his responsibilities or give up hers. Both are committed to unity of action and effort.

Oneness in marriage is not dominating or being dominated. It is unity through right cooperation of all the parts.

Marriage is a process which challenges both partners to commit to something bigger and better than either. In a one-flesh marriage both count, both belong, both are accepted, both are affirmed, both have recognized abilities, and both are affectionately appreciated. In a one-flesh marriage both win and neither loses.

In a one-flesh marriage the roles of the man and woman are different just as men and women are different. The differences need to be appreciated and valued, not rejected and devalued. Unhealthy marriages, like unhealthy families, allow one partner to devalue the other's role and contribution.

If acceptance, love, affirmation, and value pervade the marriage, they will also abound in the family. The kids will experience what Mom and Dad share with each other. Each member of the family will have a place or a role different from the others but equally valued. This creates healthy families.

In the one-flesh marriage the guidelines that make up each person's role are principles of relationship that each person may implement differently. The guidelines for the man's role or the woman's role do not change. But the two individuals' implementation of the guidelines will make their marriage healthy and unique.

It is like the Olympic figure skating competition. Each skater is required to include certain compulsory maneuvers in the routine, but how the skaters do each exercise becomes the substance of individual performance. They choose their own music, costume, and exercise sequence. Each skater will do some exercises better than others. They leave the mark of their individuality yet adhere to the basic requirements.

A one-flesh model of marriage works this way. Each partner stamps the relationship with the imprint of his or her own personality yet adheres to the basic requirements in doing so.

The description of one-flesh marriage roles comes from the Scriptures. When unbiblical relational roles and models of marriage are practiced, the following will result.

Marital Discord

Each person must agree to right role relationship to resolve marital conflict. Much unresolved conflict in marriage is due to differing expectations each person has of the other. Lack of unity, unresolved conflict, and poor intimacy can be the result of a wrong marital role stemming from a wrong model of marriage.

Using a biblical model of one-flesh marriage can resolve role expectation problems while giving clear steps to intimacy and unity of purpose. Shared values and goals produce unity and resolve discord. Ascribing to the Bible as an authority greater than ourselves provides the framework for unity in marriage.

Separation or Divorce

A lack of unity and oneness in marriage can lead to the pain of separation or divorce. This causes additional financial responsibilities, increased pressure, more loneliness, and one-sided child-care responsibilities. It also increases financial pressures, loneliness, and separation from family.

The kids suffer the most through loss and inner decisions that will have a negative impact on their future relationships.

A mutually adopted model of one-flesh marriage stresses commitment, mutual accountability, and mutual need fulfillment. Both can win; no one has to lose.

Emotionally Absent Spouse (Parent)

The lack of a one-flesh model can result in one or the other not taking the responsibility to parent the children or in one spouse not taking the responsibility to nurture the other emotionally.

Absent spouses or parents create deep wounds of rejection in the persons they were to be there for. Marriage and parenting require emotional need fulfillment.

The lack of biblical roles in a marriage creates models of marriage that don't work. One partner or the other will not take the responsibility to invest in the right way emotionally and even spiritually. This failure will produce a deep void of unmet need and rejection.

Surrogate (Substitute) Spouse or Parent

The void caused by lack of marital need fulfillment can cause the deprived spouse to meet emotional needs through one of the children. This happened in Sally's situation. She became her mother's comforter. It was as though she were the nurturing mother rather than the child to be nurtured by the parent.

I was a surrogate spouse for my mom. I helped compensate for her disappointment in Dad. I talked and shared with her when Dad didn't. As is common, their lack of one-flesh marriage affected my role in the family. The parents' lack of biblical role performance negatively affects how each person in the family relates to the others.

A surrogate spouse or parent is a setup for codependency. The child, when grown, will look for needy people to marry or care for because the child has learned a role and identity of getting needs met through meeting the needs of others. This is why so many people in the helping professions are codependent. Most have come from families in which they were the surrogate spouse or parent.

Passive Son

The problem of traditional and reversed marriages has created a whole generation of passive men—men who are confused about their roles and behave passively in the marriage. They have made inner vows and judgments against Dad. This has caused them, by extension, to judge against themselves. They lack confidence, don't want to be like Dad, but don't know how else to be.

They relate better to women than men because Mom talked to them and raised them, Dad didn't. They will have difficulty not being under the control or authority of women because they are used to being under Mom's control. Once again, she raised them, Dad didn't. This can also make them resent women. If sex gets mixed into the equation, they will give love to get sex and seldom be responsible in the relationship. Sex will become the safe way of making contact with women. Opening up his heart and life to a woman will be too fearful a thing to do. He will choose a reversed or negotiated marriage model.

Victimized Daughter

The lack of right role models creates a wound in the daughter against her dad and mom. She will have difficulty trusting men because her father did not meet her or her mother's emotional needs. Or if he met hers and not her mom's, she will be in competition with Mom for Dad's approval.

Either way, she will end up with a high need for affection, attention, and approval from men. She will idolize men and then despise herself or them when they fail her. Or she will reject men, not trusting them. Control will be a big issue in her life. She will not want to be controlled by a man. She will fear it too much and will always take control of relationships to try to get her needs met.

She will wrestle with men to get her intimacy needs met and will choose a negotiated or reversed marriage model and run the risk of being codependent.

Codependency is a new term for an old problem of not loving, caring, or giving rightly in relationships. The marriage relationship is the key one upon which all others pivot. Healthy marriages will make healthy families capable of preventing codependent relationship patterns.

I want to emphasize again, codependency begins in the need fulfillment of family life. Family life is controlled by Mom and Dad and their marriage relationship. The health of the family is directly proportional to the health of the marriage. Preventing codependency requires a healthy marriage relationship. If the marriage isn't working well, the other family relationships rarely work well—the emotional and relational needs don't get fulfilled in healthy ways. This imprints wrong patterns of getting needs met in relationship. The children carry these wrong inner imprints into their relationships with others, repeating the unhealthiness in their generation.

To escape the vicious cycle of negative imprint and repetition, resolve to work on your marriage issues. Honestly look at which model of marriage you've learned or are living. Settle in your own conscience before God what you believe His will is for your marriage and life. And pray. A healthy marriage requires great courage to face our needs, weaknesses, and responsibilities as well as those of the other person. It also requires His empowerment. The willingness and power to lead a fruitful life of healthy love comes from deep within our spirits. Pray that God's Holy Spirit will enable you to accomplish this desired result.

Chapter 15

God is our refuge and strength,
A very present help in trouble. . . .
Cease striving and know
that I am God. . . .
The LORD of hosts is with us;
The God of Jacob is
our stronghold.
Psalm 46:1, 10–11 (NASB)

15 Who Is Your God?

THE SKIRT WAS SHORT and tight, her blouse partially unbuttoned. She was obviously braless. Her long black hair swung down, covering her shoulders. Her appearance belied her mere eighteen years. As she sat down in my office, I was struck by how seductive yet pretty she was. There was no doubt in my mind that she knew men and what they wanted. I asked her how I might help. Refusing to look at me, she stared down at her foot, one eye partially hidden by her flowing hair.

"Bud is going to leave me if I don't get counseling."

"Why would he want to leave you?"

"He caught me fooling around with his friend."

"What do you mean by fooling around?" I asked.

"Bud caught us having sex." The bluntness of the answer surprised me.

"Do you love Bud?"

"Yes. That's why I did it."

I was puzzled. "You had sex with his friend because you love Bud?"

"Every time he hurts me I get back by fooling around."

Now I understood. "How many times has this happened?"

"Maybe ten or twelve."

"Does Bud know about all of them?"

"No."

"What were you hoping I could do for you?"

"Nothing."

Legs crossed, she pumped her foot up and down while she hunched in the corner of the couch. As far away from me as possible, it is the spot where most clients sit when they need to feel safe. Her eyes were still downcast.

I asked, "Why did you come if I can't help you?"

"Because Bud made me."

"And if I can't help you, how are you going to work this out with Bud?"

Finally the tears began to run down her tan cheeks, dropping unchecked on her chest as she remained immobile. After a long silence she replied, "I'm cursed. No one can help me."

"Tell me how you're cursed."

"I'm no good. I have bad blood in me. I'm just like my mother."

"What was your mother like?"

"She was no good. She was a whore who liked men and booze too much. I was adopted out and raised by white parents. I like men and partying just like my mother."

Of American Indian descent, Norine had been raised from age ten by a couple who had adopted her as their own. Almost defiantly she continued, "You don't know what I'm like and what I've done. I've slept with more men than you could count, and I've been married twice already. But Bud is different." As some of her anger left, the tears started again. "Bud treats me nice. He doesn't beat me or use me."

Now the tears were torrential, and my own eyes began to fill as I felt her pain. She was trapped by her own self-defeating ways and knew of no way out. I asked, "Have you ever asked God to help you change?"

Her soft "No" was muffled by the sound of crying.

I began to read to her from Psalm 23, the verses punctuated by her sobs:

> The LORD is my shepherd;
> I shall not want.
> He makes me to lie down in green pastures. . . .

As I finished with the words "And I will dwell in the house of the LORD forever," she stood up and walked out of my office without looking at me or saying anything. I thought about her during the week, hoping she would come back and begin her journey to healing.

A week later I walked into my reception room to greet the next client. She was a vivacious, dark-haired young woman, glowing with radiance and grace, attractively dressed and very pleasant. I introduced myself and asked her to have a seat in my office. Turning to the receptionist I asked who the new client was.

She quickly said to me, "I didn't recognize her either. It's Norine."

"Norine who?" I asked.

"The girl you saw last week," she replied.

"It can't be," I argued.

"Well, it is, and she's waiting for you," my receptionist said firmly.

I retreated into my office, closing the door behind me. I must have been staring because she asked, "Is it okay that I came back?"

"Of course," I assured her. "It's just that you don't look the same and I didn't recognize you at first. You've changed."

She smiled and told me the story. As I had read the twenty-third psalm to her, she pictured in her mind the green pastures dotted with many sheep and a shepherd. When I reached "He makes me to lie down in green pastures," she saw the shepherd walk over to a lamb alone—bloodied, bruised, angry, with matted and dirty fleece. The shepherd reached down, picked up the battered lamb, and began to mend its wounds and clean its coat. The lamb struggled to be free of the tender ministrations, but the shepherd smiled and kept on until the lamb was healthy, its wool white as snow. The shepherd then held the lamb close, speaking tender words of love and care.

The image was so powerful she left my office to be alone to sort out the experience. In the parking lot she sobbed for over an hour while she basked in the shepherd's love. She was the lamb in the psalm, and Jesus was the shepherd.

The experience had so profoundly touched her it had changed her attitude and very appearance. She was no longer the old Norine but was now different. The shame of her mother, her birth, three rapes, physical abuse, and countless men was now cleansed from her life. She felt different because she was—and she knew it! The love had changed her. She had never encountered such potent feelings of love, forgiveness, and acceptance.

Norine's story is indelibly etched in my mind. Though it happened years ago, I doubt that I will ever forget it. It was a dramatic illustration of the power of Jesus' love. I invariably remember it whenever the subject of who God is comes up.

Just after I finished the final seminar session for a special weekend, Carolyn stood in front of me with that intense look she gets when she is absorbed in thought and blurted out, "Who is your God? I want to get to know Him. I've been a Christian for years but have never heard someone share who God is like you did. It made me realize that I have seen Him as stern and distant, not a personal, loving God like yours."

The phrase has stuck with me all these years. I often reminisce about who my God is to myself as well as others. I like challenging people with the question "Who is your God?" It really makes them think. It also makes many of them realize they don't really know the answer or how much love they are missing in not knowing Jesus.

The New-Age movement has stirred people lacking deep spiritual roots to reexamine their need for spiritual experience. *Time* magazine has reported a renewed interest in spirituality sweeping our country.

Spirituality is what God is all about. The inner part of all of us yearns for something that will transcend the pressures and problems of this life. The New-Age experiences of channeling and crystal power appeal to the need for spiritual awakening. As our society has become more complex and pressured, our need for the deep peace, security, and significance that spirituality can bring has increased.

Addiction, like codependence, is a spiritual problem. Each is an attempt at fulfilling innermost needs for love, peace, and significance. Only the power of a spiritual awakening can quench these needs. Alcoholics Anonymous has been recognized as the single most effective answer to addiction ever devised because it is a spiritual program of recovery. The twelve steps are all spiritually directed toward God and recovery. The twelfth step sums it all up: "Having had a spiritual awakening as the result of these steps, we try to carry this message to alcoholics, and to practice these principles in all our affairs."

The essential ingredient of all the anonymous programs such as AA, GA, OA, NA, EA is the spiritual component. An addict has relinquished the self-control to a substance. Addiction is a failure to control. The key question in life is who is in control of you? Whatever controls you will rule your life. Whatever you use to comfort you and bring you inner fulfillment will control you, and you can become addicted—whether the focal motivation is fame, power, love, or glory.

The World Health Organization defines addiction as a mood-altering event, experience, or thing that has life-damaging consequences. The bottom line with addictions is that they are used to alter our feelings. We use them to make us feel better—however fleetingly—to bring peace, love, and fulfillment to our inner being. As the period of euphoria becomes shorter, we require more and more to maintain the good feelings.

The problem is that addictions are progressive. The more of something you use to control your emotions, the more of it you'll need to sustain the feelings. The more you drink to feel good, the more you consume to keep feeling good. Said one dying alcoholic, "My liquid comfort has proven to be poison."

Addictions also lead to mental, emotional, physical, and spiritual death. Anything you hand power over to becomes your controller, and once you've lost control, your self-worth and self-respect are also damaged. Ultimately you end up in a war with yourself, one in which you're the loser. This battle can kill you emotionally and spiritually—sometimes even result in physical death.

Sexual addictions, like eating, drug, and alcohol addictions, bring physical consequences. AIDS is now a serious threat. Many drug abusers and alcoholics meet an untimely death. Food disorders such as anorexia and bulimia can also kill. We fail to realize that most domestic violence and love murders are due to relational addictions.

Another problem with addictions is the insatiable craving that develops, making it impossible for us to function without a steady supply. The desire can become so overwhelming that we will risk serious consequences to keep it fed.

On vacation last year, Susan and I ran across a newspaper article relating the apprehension at Yellowstone Park of a man who was hiding in the underground septic tank of an outdoor latrine. Wrapped in plastic, he was watching women as they used the toilet. It was his absurd attempt to satisfy his voyeuristic addiction.

Addicts are like this, going to nearly any length to feed the addiction. Codependents are well known for abusing themselves and going to extreme lengths to get someone to love them. This is the power an addiction has over the life of anyone who flirts with meeting deep emotional and spiritual needs through a mood-altering event, experience, person, or thing.

We are spiritual beings who require a spiritual awakening to meet the deepest needs of our existence. True inner peace and significance come from spirituality, not people, experiences, or things.

The danger in this is that the brand of spirituality we choose can be harmful instead of helpful. Our counseling center specializes in spiritually related problems. We get referrals from all over the United States and Canada, even Mexico at times. Most come because they want healing for their hurt. Many also come because they have practiced a brand of spirituality that is now causing pain, fear, and bondage instead of power, freedom, and healing.

A common symptom pattern of those who have dabbled with the wrong kind of spirituality is fear, nightmares, heart palpitations, chest pains, and panic attacks. Others are afflicted with torment, anxiety, and worry. Still others become moody and depressed and feel harassed.

Most of these symptoms, while also applying to anxiety disorders caused by other problems, have a spiritual cause. They come from occult practices of divination, satanic rituals, seances, channeling, and the use of both black and white magic. While each of these can provide a spiritual experience, the long-term effects are negative. They normally inculcate fear, anxiety, and torment rather than peace, love, and fulfillment.

What you decide about who your God is will determine who controls your life and even its ultimate outcome. My God is Jesus. No other. I have come to believe in Him because I have consistently found that His presence in my life brings healing, peace, and joy. I have watched countless individuals like Norine leave my office healed from their wounds, delivered from their fears, and more secure because of Him. Many still need to walk a long path to resolve the past, but God becomes the stable and enabling source of well-being.

I have found that He is the one who mends the broken heart and sets the captive free. Truth is not an abstract concept but a person. Jesus Christ.

Codependents are wounded people, needing the love, affirmation, and acceptance only Jesus can bring. When we are able to surrender our hearts to Him, He lovingly heals them. The healing can come in a moment of experienced love as it did for Norine. Or it can come through repeated assurances. Either way, it is there for the asking.

My codependency has been profoundly released through His love. My understanding of codependency and the healing I have experienced and witnessed have come through Him.

Codependency *is* a wounded heart's cry for His love. It is

a vain attempt to recover what was never given us in life and is now available through Him. It's trying to give, care, and love out of our strength rather than His.

Codependency reflects our failure to enter fully into His love. The ones we love, care for, or give too much to for all the wrong reasons are also love-starved. They need His love before they will respond rightly to ours.

Jesus is every codependent's answer to loving another more than you are loved. Jesus offers the only one-way relationship that is healthy. He will always love us more than we love Him. His is the only love offered purely and consistently, with no strings attached.

". . . the same, yesterday, today and forever!"

About the Author

ALFRED ELLS is a counselor and the director of Samaritan Counseling Services in Scottsdale, Arizona. His years of counseling experience, healing, consultation, and training are also directed toward equipping laypersons, pastoral staff, and other counselors to meet the needs of others effectively.

He is broadly educated, receiving a Bachelor of Science degree from the University of Arizona and a Master of Counseling from Arizona State University. He is a graduate of the Mental Health Administration Continuing Education program for Tulane University.

His professional credentials include being a director for *I Care* Prison Ministries, House of Hope, Community of Living Water Teaching Center, El Shaddai Ministries International, Southwestern Center for Behavioral Health Studies, Community Organization for Drug Abuse, Mental Health and Alcohol, The New Foundation, and the *Journal of Mental Health*. He has been chairperson for the State Committee for Certification of Human Services Workers and program planner for the Arizona Conference on Human Services Workers.

He works with corporate, religious, and individual clients. He has written for publications and continues to write from his experience in bringing individuals to wholeness.

Known for his wisdom and insightful teaching, Al Ells "is kindness and caring in shoe leather. He walks in practical and personal ways with his family, friends, staff, and clients— and with his God."